Level 2 Diploma for IT Users
for City & Guilds

Databases

Level

2

Susan Ward

Endorsed by

City&
Guilds

www.heinemann.co.uk
✓ Free online support
✓ Useful weblinks
✓ 24 hour online ordering

01865 888058

Heinemann

Inspiring generations

Heinemann Educational Publishers
Halley Court, Jordan Hill, Oxford OX2 8EJ
Part of Harcourt Education

Heinemann is the registered trademark of
Harcourt Education Limited

© Susan Ward 2003

First published 2003

08 07 06 05 04 03
10 9 8 7 6 5 4 3 2 1

British Library Cataloguing in Publication Data is available
from the British Library on request.

ISBN 0 435 46279 2

Publisher's note
The materials in this Work have been developed by Harcourt Education and the
content and the accuracy are the sole responsibility of Harcourt Education. The City
and Guilds of London Institute accepts no liability howsoever in respect of any
breach of the intellectual property rights of any third party howsoever occasioned or
damage to the third party's property or person as a result of the use of this Work.

The City & Guilds name and logo are the registered trade marks of The City and
Guilds of London Institute and are used under licence.

Typeset by Tech-Set Ltd, Gateshead, Tyne and Wear
Printed in the UK by Thomson Litho Ltd.

Acknowledgements
The screenshots in this book are reprinted with permission from the Microsoft
Corporation.

Tel: 01865 888058 www.heinemann.co.uk

Contents

Introduction

City & Guilds e-Quals is an exciting new range of IT qualifications developed with leading industry experts. These comprehensive, progressive awards cover everything from getting to grips with basic IT to gaining the latest professional skills.

The range consists of both User and Practitioner qualifications. User qualifications (Levels 1–3) are ideal for those who use IT as part of their job or in life generally, while Practitioner qualifications (Levels 2–3) have been developed for those who need to boost their professional skills in, for example, networking or software development.

e-Quals boasts online testing and a dedicated website with news and support materials and web-based training. The qualifications reflect industry standards and meet the requirements of the National Qualifications Framework.

With e-Quals you will not only develop your expertise, you will gain a qualification that is recognised by employers all over the world.

Level 2 Databases is one of the units making up the City & Guilds e-Quals Diploma for IT Users.

The database unit is organised into seven outcomes.

You will learn to:
- apply database concepts
- create and modify a database structure
- create and use a data entry form
- maintain a database
- sort and index a database
- carry out single and multiple condition searches
- create and modify a report, and produce hard copy output.

The outcomes matching guide, near the end of the book, gives the outcomes in full and relates each learning point to the section of the book where it is covered. Your tutor will give you a copy of the outcomes, so that you can sign and date each learning point as you master the skills and knowledge.

Before starting work on Databases Level 2, you should have completed Databases Level 1, or have equivalent experience of using Microsoft Access.

Each section of this book contains information and practical tasks. There is a detailed method to guide you when you first learn to carry out each task. At the end of a section you will have a chance to practise your skills, check your knowledge, or both. Consolidation exercises provide further practice. Finally you will be able to complete practice assignments, which cover a range of skills and are designed to be similar in style to the City & Guilds assignment for the unit.

There are some solutions to the skills practice and check your knowledge questions at the end of the book. There is also a quick reference section giving methods of carrying out common tasks.

You will need to start at the beginning of the book and work through the sections in order, because tasks in later sections use databases that are created in earlier sections.

In order to give detailed methods for each task it is necessary to refer to a specific database application and operating system, though the City & Guilds unit is not specific and can be completed using any database application and operating system. This book refers to Microsoft Access 2000, which is the database application in the Microsoft Office 2000 suite, and to Microsoft Windows 95/98/ME.

Section 1 | Database tables

You will

- Describe databases and database software
- Create a database table structure
- Use and describe data types: text, number, currency and date/time
- Use and describe the logical data type
- Enter data into a table
- Print the contents of a table
- Describe the importance of file management and back up
- Make backup copies of a database file

Information: Databases and database software

As you will know from Level 1 or from your previous experience, a **database** is a collection of organised data. Many databases are now held on computer systems. They are managed by database applications or database management systems. One database application is Microsoft Access. The application allows the database user to enter new data, alter or delete data and to process data in a variety of ways. Data can quickly be selected, sorted and presented on the screen or on paper. Computerised databases have become vital to many organisations.

An Access database has one or more **tables.** A table stores data in the form of **records**, one record in each row of the table. Each record holds data about one item of interest. The item could be a person, such as an employee, a customer or a club member. It could be an object such as a book, a video or a component in a warehouse. It could be something more abstract such as an appointment, a theatre booking or a holiday. A record is divided into **fields**. An employee record might have fields for surname, forename, payroll number, and so on. The columns of a table have **field names** as headings. All the records in a table should hold data about the same sort of item. If the organisation needs to store data about customers and about videos then there should be separate tables for customers and for videos. Access is able to manage linked tables as a **relational database**, but linked tables are not covered at Level 2.

Information: Health and safety

Keep health and safety issues in mind as you continue with your computer work. These issues, which are fully covered in the City & Guilds e-Quals IT Principles units, include:

- Electrical safety
- The design and layout of the work area, furniture and equipment
- Good working habits.

As you work, check your posture, check your keyboarding technique, and remember to take regular breaks away from the computer.

Information: The tasks in Section 1

You should already know how to manage files and folders on the computer system you are using. You should be able to design, create and save a database table structure containing fields of different data types. You should be able to enter and maintain records and print out the contents of the table. The Section 1 tasks give you some practice with these familiar activities, and also introduce a new data type: the **logical** or **Boolean** type.

Task 1.1 Create a database table structure

Method

1. Start up Microsoft Access.
2. When the Microsoft Access starting dialogue box appears, choose to create a blank Access database.
3. Give your new database the filename **Courses.mdb**.
4. Choose to create a table in design view.
5. Enter field names and data types as shown below. For each field, enter the field size or format in the lower part of the design window.

Field name	Data type	Field size/format
Course name	Text	30
Level	Text	20
Sessions	Number	Long Integer
Start date	Date/Time	Medium date
Price	Currency	Automatic 2 decimal places

Table 1.1 Structure of the Courses table

6. Save the table structure as Courses (Your name). Do not allow Access to create a primary key.

Hint:

Include your own name in the names of all tables that you create during your City & Guilds work. When you print the table, your name will appear at the top of the paper as part of the table name. You need to have your name on your work if you are sharing a printer.

Information: Data types – text, number, currency and date/time

- The **Text** data type can hold any combination of characters: letters, numbers, punctuation marks and spaces. The field size is the number of characters the field can store. It should be chosen so that there is room for the longest entry that is likely to occur. The maximum size is 255 characters. Longer text entries can be stored in a memo field.
- The **Number** data type is for numbers only. Mixtures of numbers and other characters should be stored as text. Phone numbers needing a leading zero, e.g. 0123512345, should be stored as text. Whole numbers are stored as Integer or Long Integer field size. Numbers with a fractional or decimal part are stored as Single or →

Double field size, and can be formatted to show a fixed number of decimal places.

- The **Currency** data type is a specialised form of number, optimised for efficient calculation. By default it shows a currency symbol and 2 decimal places.
- The **Date/Time** data type can be formatted to show dates in long, medium or short form, and time in various forms.
- The **Autonumber** data type automatically enters a Long Integer so that each record has a unique number.

Information: The logical data type

The **logical** or **Boolean** data type may be new to you. It appears in the Access list of data types as **Yes/No**. A field with the logical data type holds a value of either True or False. Access can display a True value as True, Yes, On or –1, or it can show a check box with a tick in it. Access can display a False value as False, No, Off or 0, or it can display a check box without a tick. Whatever is displayed, the value that Access actually stores is either –1, meaning True, or 0, meaning False.

Task 1.2   Use the logical data type

Method

1   You should still have the design of your table on the screen. Key in an additional field name: **Evening**. This field will show whether or not a course is held in the evening.
2   In the Data Type column, select Yes/No as the data type for the Evening field.
3   Leave the default Yes/No format in the field properties in the lower part of the window.
4   Save the table structure again.

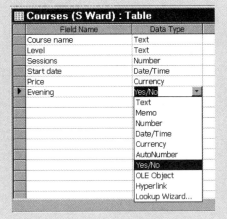

Figure 1.1 The logical Yes/No data type

Task 1.3　Enter data into a table

Method

1 Change to datasheet view of the table by using the toolbar View button.
2 Notice that the Evening field shows a check box. When you make entries in the Evening field you should put a tick in the box for True or leave the box unticked for False.
3 Enter records as shown:

Course name	Level	Sessions	Start date	Price	Evening
Introduction to MS Word	Beginner	10	24-Sep-02	£50.00	True
Introduction to MS Word	Beginner	11	25-Sep-02	£50.00	False
Starting MS Excel	Beginner	11	23-Sep-02	£50.00	False
Starting Publisher	Beginner	10	16-Sep-02	£60.00	True
Using Publisher	Intermediate	15	09-Sep-02	£65.00	True
MS Word at Work	Intermediate	20	11-Sep-02	£70.00	True
MS Word Expert	Advanced	4	11-Oct-02	£80.00	False
MS Excel Expert	Advanced	4	14-Oct-02	£80.00	False

Table 1.2 Data for the Courses table

4 Widen fields as necessary so that all the data is showing. Save the table structure after widening fields.

Information: Faster data entry

You can use the mouse to click in a check box and place or remove a tick. Rather than taking your hand away from the keyboard, you may find the following method quicker. Use the Tab key or the Enter key to move into the field containing the check box. Press the spacebar to place or remove a tick

Sometimes a field contains data that is the same as the data in the field immediately above it. For example, several records have the word 'Beginner' in the Level field. Instead of keying in the data again, you can use a keyboard shortcut. Hold down the Ctrl key as you press the single apostrophe key ('). This will copy data from the field above.

Hint:

Remember that there is no need to save records when you have entered them. Access automatically saves each record as you move out of it. You do need to save any changes you make to the structure of a table.

Task 1.4 — Print the contents of a table

Method

1	Print preview the table using the toolbar button or the File menu Print Preview option.
2	You may find that there is not room to display all the fields on one sheet of paper. Change to landscape orientation. (Use the File menu and select the Page Setup option. Click the Page tab and choose Landscape.)
3	Print the table in landscape orientation.
4	Close the table and close down Access.

Information: File management and back up

Access stores a whole database in one file even if the database has several tables, queries and other objects. Some other database management packages store each table, query, and so on in a separate file. It is important to keep these files together in a folder. Files should be named to show the contents and the file type. Access organises tables, queries, etc. for you within the database file, but it is still important to give a descriptive name to each database object.

In Level 1 you learned the importance of making regular backup copies of database files so that a damaged or lost database can be restored. You will be using small databases that can be backed up onto a floppy disk. Commercial databases are much bigger and would need to be backed up to another medium such as CD-RW, tape or a second hard disk.

Task 1.5 — Make backup copies of a database file

Method

1	Find and open the folder containing your Courses.mdb file.
2	Create a second folder called **AccessBackup**.
3	Copy your Courses.mdb file into the new folder.
4	Change the name of this copy of the file to **CoursesBackup.mdb**.
5	If you have a floppy disk, create a folder called **AccessBackup2** on the floppy disk.
6	Make another backup copy of your database file in this folder on the floppy disk. Give this backup copy a name that identifies it as a backup copy of Courses.mdb

Remember:

Take regular breaks away from the computer.

→ Practise your skills 1.1: Books database

You are asked to create a database table to hold records of books for sale. You will be given a sample of data, and part of your task is to plan a suitable table structure.

You will need this database later, so carry out the practice even if you are confident about the methods.

1 Look at the sample of data that follows. Field names are given at the top of the columns. Decide what data types and field sizes or formats would be suitable to store the data.

Stock No	Author	Title	Price	Year_Published	Hardback
21	Jane Austen	Emma	£2.50	1985	No
22	Kazuo Ishiguro	The Unconsoled	£7.99	1995	No
23	Miss Read	Life at Thrush Green	£9.99	1984	No
24	Louis de Bernieres	Captain Corelli's Mandolin	£6.99	1998	No
25	Vikram Seth	A Suitable Boy	£15.99	1993	Yes
26	Jane Austen	Pride and Prejudice	£2.99	1988	No
27	Charles Dickens	Oliver Twist	£18.00	2000	Yes
28	Daniel Defoe	Robinson Crusoe	£15.00	1960	Yes
29	Jane Austen	Sense and Sensibility	£2.50	1980	No
30	Jane Austen	Persuasion	£2.50	1980	No
31	Kazuo Ishiguro	The Remains of the Day	£6.99	1993	No
32	Charles Dickens	David Copperfield	£18.00	1975	Yes
33	Charles Dickens	The Pickwick Papers	£17.00	1982	Yes

Table 1.3 Data for the Books table

2 On paper, write down a design for a database table to store the data. Arrange your design in three columns, like the design for the Courses table in Table 1.1.

Field name	Data type	Field size/format

Table 1.4 Structure of the Books table

3 Start up Access and create a new database called **Books.mdb**.

4 Create a new table in design view. Enter the field names, and enter your chosen data type and field size or format for each field. Save the table with the name **Books (Your name)**. Do not let Access add a primary key.

5 Enter the sample data from Table 1.3.

6 Adjust field widths as necessary to display all the data, and save the table structure again.

7 Print the table on one sheet of paper.

8 Close the table and close down Access.

9 Make a backup copy of your Books.mdb file in your AccessBackup folder. Give the copied file a name that shows it is a backup copy of the Books database.

→ Practise your skills 1.2: Seeds database

You are asked to create a database table to hold records of packets of seeds for sale. You will be given a sample of data, and part of your task is to plan a suitable table structure.

You will need this database later, so carry out the practice even if you are confident about the methods.

1   Look at the sample of data that follows. Field names are given at the top of the columns. Decide what data types and field sizes or formats would be suitable to store the data.

Cat No	Name	Price	Available	Type	Height (cm)
AX0293	Alyssum	£1.29	Yes	HA	8
AX0298	Snapdragon Delice	£1.99	Yes	HHA	30
AX0299	Snapdragon Hobbit	£2.49	Yes	HHA	20
AX0320	Aquilegia Winky	£2.99	Yes	HP	40
AX0321	Aquilegia Petticoats	£1.99	Yes	HP	90
AX0334	Aster Pink Fizz	£1.49	Yes	HHA	20
AX0335	Aster Blue Magic	£0.99	Yes	HHA	80
AX0336	Aster Pink Magic	£0.99	No	HHA	60

Table 1.5 Data for the Seeds table

2   On paper, write down a design for a database table to store the data. Arrange your design in three columns headed Field name, Data type and Field size/format.

3   Start up Access and create a new database called **Seeds.mdb**.

4   Create a new table in design view. Enter the field names, and enter your chosen data type and field size or format for each field. Save the table with the name **Seeds (Your name)**. Do not let Access add a primary key.

5   Enter the sample data from Table 1.5.

6   Adjust field widths as necessary to display all the data, and save the table structure again.

7   Print the table on one sheet of paper.

8   Close the table and close down Access.

9   Make a backup copy of your Seeds.mdb file in your AccessBackup folder. Give the copied file a name that shows it is a backup copy of the Seeds database.

→ Check your knowledge

1 One row of a table contains one ...

2 Where do the field names appear in datasheet view of a table?

3 A record consists of several ...

4 Which data type would you choose for a field that is to hold names of towns?

5 Which data type and field size would you choose to hold whole numbers?

6 Which data type and field size would you choose to hold numbers with a fractional part, such as 23.54, 109.3?

7 Which data type and field size or format would you choose to hold sums of money to be shown as pounds and pence?

8 Which data type and field size or format would you choose to hold dates in the form 12-Aug-02?

9 Which data type would you choose to hold values that must be either true or false?

10 Which data type would you choose if you want your records automatically numbered for you?

Section 2

Changing table structure and contents

You will learn to

- Open an existing database
- Display records and fields and edit data
- Modify a database structure by inserting a new field
- Delete an existing field
- Find and replace the contents of fields
- Modify the data type of suitable existing fields
- Modify the attributes or properties of the data type of suitable existing fields
- Save and print database structures
- Copy and modify table structures within the same database file
- Copy a complete table, structure and data, within a database file
- Append data from one table to another, within a database file
- Export a complete table to a different database file
- Export a table structure to a different database file
- Copy and paste records from one table to another

In this section you will use the Courses database that you created in Section 1. You will look at the existing data in the Courses table and make changes to the data. This sort of activity is likely to be carried out frequently by database users. You will also make changes to the structure of the table, adding fields, deleting fields and altering field properties. Structural changes are not likely to be carried out often. You will also copy records from one table to another and from one database to another.

Task 2.1   Open an existing database

You will open the Courses database that you created in Section 1.

Method

I	Start Access.
2	Recently used databases are listed in the 'Open an Existing File' section of the Microsoft Access starting dialogue box. If your Courses database is listed then click to select it and click OK. If it is not listed then click on More Files . . . and click OK. Use the Open dialogue box to navigate to the Courses.mdb file and open it.
3	The database window of the Courses database should appear.

Task 2.2 — Display records and fields and edit data

Method

1. Select the Courses table in the database window. To open the table in datasheet view you can either double click on the Courses table name, or you can click on the Open button at the top of the database window.
2. The table should appear, displaying the data that you entered in Section 1.
3. Change the starting date of the Starting Publisher course to 23-Sep-02.
4. Change the price of the Starting MS Excel course to £55.

Task 2.3 — Modify a database structure by inserting a new field

You will add an extra field between the Course name and the Level fields. The new field will show the site where the course is held.

Method

1. Switch to design view of the Courses table by using the View button on the toolbar.
2. Click into the Level field.
3. Click on the Insert menu and select Rows from the drop down list. A new row should appear.
4. In the new row, enter the field name **Site**.
5. Move across to the data type column, and keep text as the data type.
6. In the lower part of the window, change the field size to 20.
7. Save the table design by clicking the Save icon on the toolbar.
8. Switch to datasheet view using the View button on the toolbar.
9. Enter data into the new field as follows:

Course name	Site
Introduction to MS Word	Community Centre
Introduction to MS Word	Main site
Starting MS Excel	Community Centre
Starting Publisher	Main site
Using Publisher	Main site
MS Word at Work	Main site
MS Word Expert	Main site
MS Excel Expert	Main site

Table 2.1 Data for the Site field

Task 2.4 | Delete an existing field

The Level field is no longer needed. You will delete it.

Hint:

An alternative way of deleting a field is to click in the left margin of the row so that the whole row is highlighted. You can then use the Delete key on the keyboard.

Method

1. Switch back to the design view of the table.
2. Click into the Level field.
3. Click on the Edit menu and select Delete Rows from the drop down list, or click the Delete Rows button on the toolbar.
4. You should see a warning message asking if you want to delete the field, and reminding you that you will lose all the data in the field. The data cannot be recovered if you go ahead. Click Yes to confirm that you want to delete the field. Save the table design.

Task 2.5 | Find and replace the contents of fields

The organiser of part-time courses has decided to change the name of the Introduction to MS Word course to Starting MS Word. The main site has been given the name of Riverside. Your Courses table is very small and it would be quite easy to replace the entries by keying in the new data. Commercial database tables are usually very large, so you need a better method of finding and replacing entries.

Method

Replacing entries one at a time

1. Open the Courses table in datasheet view.
2. Click into the Course name column. This is the field you are going to search.
3. Click on the Edit menu and select Replace from the drop down list.
4. The Find and Replace dialogue box should appear, with the Replace tab in front.

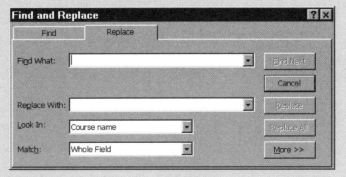

Figure 2.1 The Find and Replace dialogue box

5. In the Find What box, key in: **Introduction to MS Word**. The text you type in here must exactly match the text you are searching for in the field.
6. In the Replace With box, key in: **Starting MS Word**.

7 Check that the Look In box displays **Course name**. This is the field that you want to search. The alternative is to search the entire table. You can see this alternative if you click the arrow at the right of the Look In box and display the drop down list. Keep Course name displayed in the box when you close the drop down list.

8 Check that the Match box displays **Whole Field**. The alternatives in the drop down list are Any part of Field and Start of Field.

9 Click the Find Next button. One of the **Introduction to MS Word** entries should be selected in the table.

10 Click the Replace button. The entry should be replaced, and the next **Introduction to MS Word** entry should be selected.

11 Click the Replace button again. The entry should be replaced.

12 There are no more entries to find. Click the Replace button again and you should see an error message saying 'Microsoft Access can't find the text you specified in the Find What box'. Click OK to close the message box.

13 Click the Cancel button to close the Find and Replace dialogue box.

Replacing several entries at once

14 Click into the Site column. This is the field to be searched next.

15 Click on the Edit menu and select Replace from the drop down list. The Find and Replace dialogue box should appear as before.

16 In the Find What box, key in: **Main site**.

17 In the Replace With box, key in: **Riverside**.

18 Check that the Look In box displays **Site**.

19 Check that the Match box displays **Whole Field**.

20 Click the Replace All button. You should see a warning message saying that you will not be able to undo this replace operation. Click Yes to confirm that you want to continue.

21 Look at the table. All the Main site entries should have been changed to Riverside.

More replace options

22 Click the More button to show an extra part of the Find and Replace dialogue box.

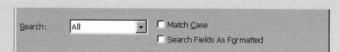

Figure 2.2 More of the Find and Replace dialogue box

23 Click the arrow to show the drop down list in the Search box. Starting from your current position in the table, you can search up or down, or you can search the whole table. Click the arrow again to close the drop down list.

24 By default, searching is not **case sensitive**. It does not matter whether letters are capitals (upper case) or not capitals (lower case). If you click the Match Case box to place a tick, Access will search for an exact match, including whether letters are capital or not.

25 The Search Fields As Formatted box is best left unticked. It applies mainly to number fields. Normally you can search for 23/9/02 and find 23-Sep-02, which is the same date but in a different format. If the box is ticked, then only entries with exactly the right format will be found. Searching is slower than normal.

26 Click the Cancel button to close the Find and Replace dialogue box.

27 Close the table and close down Access.

Hint:

Use the Replace All option with great caution. It may replace more than you intend, and it can be very difficult to correct any problems. It is usually fairly safe to Replace All if you are looking in only one field and matching the whole field. Matching any part of a field is more risky.

Information: Changing data types

You should plan database tables carefully before you create them, so that there is no need to change the data type of a field after the table structure has been created. There can be problems if you change a data type after entering data into a field. Occasionally there may be a change in the user's requirements or in the data that needs to be stored, so that a change of data type cannot be avoided.

The two most basic data types are Text and Number. Date/Time, Currency and even Yes/No are specialised kinds of Number. You can often convert between different Number types, though you may lose some data if you convert to a type that uses less storage space. Number types can generally be converted to text. Text cannot generally be converted to Number, because Number types cannot store letters, spaces or punctuation.

If Access is unable to convert between data types, or if there is a possibility of losing data, then you should see a warning message when you try to save your change of type. At this stage you can decide not to go ahead with the change.

Task 2.6	Modify the data type of suitable existing fields

You will create an extra field that can be used for experimenting with changing data types. If anything goes wrong, your other fields should not be affected.

Method

1. In design view of the Courses table, add an extra field called **Full**.
2. The data type should be text, and the field size can be left at the default size of 50. Save the table design.
3. Switch to datasheet view and enter data in the new field as shown.

Course name	Full
Starting MS Word	F
Starting MS Word	F
Starting MS Excel	N
Starting Publisher	N
Using Publisher	F
MS Word at Work	N
MS Word Expert	F
MS Excel Expert	N

Table 2.2 Data for Full field

Text to Memo and Memo to Text

4   Switch back to design view of the table.

5   Change the type of the Full field to Memo. Save the table design.

6   Switch to datasheet view. The data should be unchanged.

7   Switch back to design view and change the data type back to Text. Save the table design.

8   You should see a warning message 'Some data may be lost'. As none of the records has an entry of more than 255 characters, you should not lose any data this time. Click Yes to confirm the saved change.

9   Check in datasheet view that the entries are unchanged.

Text to Number and Number to Text

10   In design view, change the data type of the Full field to Number. Save the table design.

11   You should see a more alarming warning message, 'Microsoft Access encountered errors while converting the data. The contents of fields in 8 record(s) were deleted'. It would be wise to click No at this point, but we are experimenting, so click Yes.

12   Switch to datasheet view and look at the Full field. The field contents have indeed been deleted. You cannot store text in a number field.

13   Enter numbers in the Full field. Use 1, 2, 3, etc.

14   Switch to design view and change the type of the Full field back to Text. Save the table design.

15   Switch to datasheet view and look at the Full field. The numbers should be there, but they are now treated as text. Have they changed from right-aligned to left-aligned?

16   Switch to design view and change the type of the Full field to Number again. Save the table design.

17   Check in datasheet view that the numbers are still there. The only time you can safely change from text to number is if the text field contains only numbers.

Number to Date/Time and Date/Time to Number

18   Switch to design view and change the type of the Full field to Date/Time. Save the table design.

19   In datasheet view, you should see that the numbers are displayed as dates. Dates are saved as numbers anyway, so that the contents of the field have not really changed, they are just displayed differently.

20   Switch to design view and change the type of the Full field back to Number. Save the table design.

21   Check in datasheet view that the numbers are displayed in their original form.

Number to Currency and Currency to Number

22   Try converting from Number to Currency and back. You should find no problems with the conversion.

Number to Yes/No and Yes/No to Number

23   Convert from Number to Yes/No. In datasheet view you should see that all the entries are shown as True, with a tick in the check box. Remove one or two of the ticks to change the entries to False.

24 Convert back from Yes/No to Number. You should find that all the numbers are now shown as –1 where the entry was True, and as 0 where the entry was False. Logical (Yes/No) fields save their values as 0 or –1, but can display their values as Yes/No, True/False, On/Off or with a check box.

Yes/No to Text

25 Convert from Number back to Yes/No and save the table design.
26 Check in datasheet view that check boxes are showing True/False.
27 In design view, convert to Text. Save the table design.
28 In datasheet view you should see that the field shows the entries as Yes or No.

Text to Yes/No

29 You are converting from text to a type that is based on numbers, so you can have problems. Leave some of the entries as Yes or No. Change some entries to Y or N.
30 In design view, convert from Text to Yes/No.
31 Save the table design. You should see a warning message that the contents of fields will be deleted. Choose Yes.
32 In datasheet view you should see that the Yes and No entries have been converted correctly to true and false values. The Y and N entries have been deleted and all show as the default value of false.

You might like to try out some other conversions. When you have finished experimenting, delete the Full field.

Information: Summary of type conversions

- You can convert numbers to text but you cannot generally convert text to numbers. The conversion only works if the text field contains nothing but numbers.

- You can convert between text and memo because memo is like an extra large text field.

- You can convert from Number to Date/Time and back because Date/Time entries are saved as numbers anyway. Date/Time is a special kind of Number. Only the display is changed.

- You can convert between Number and Currency because Currency is a special kind of Number.

- If you convert from Number to Yes/No, all 0 entries become False and all non-0 entries become True. If you convert back, False becomes 0 and True becomes –1.

- You can convert Yes/No fields to text.

- Converting from text to Yes/No is not always successful. Access can recognise the words Yes, No, True, False, On, Off. It will convert these words to the logical values of true and false. It will not recognise other words or letters such as Y, N, T, F. Anything it does not recognise will be deleted and will show as false.

Hint:

If you have text entries such as T, F that mean true and false, you could use Find and Replace to convert T to True and F to False. You could then convert the type from text to Yes/No without losing data.

Modify the attributes or properties of the data type of suitable existing fields

You will change the field sizes or formats of existing fields.

Method

Text field size

1   In design view of the table, select the Course name field. In the lower part of the window, change its field size from 30 to 40. Save the table design.

2   Change the field size back to 30. Save the table design.

3   You should see a warning message 'Some data may be lost'. If there were any entries longer than 30 characters then the extra characters would be lost, but we know that there are no such long entries, so it is safe to continue. Click Yes.

Number field size

4   In design view, create a new field called **Temporary**. Give it the Number data type and the Long Integer field size.

5   Switch to datasheet view. Enter data as follows:

Course name	Temporary
Starting MS Word	123456
Starting MS Word	11
Starting MS Excel	100
Starting Publisher	100
Using Publisher	100
MS Word at Work	100
MS Word Expert	100
MS Excel Expert	100

Table 2.3 Data for Temporary field

6   Switch to design view. Select the Temporary field. Change the field size from Long Integer to Integer. Save the table design.

7   You should see an error message, 'Microsoft Access encountered errors...'. Integer is a smaller field size than Long Integer and it cannot store the number 123456. If you go ahead with the change, the number will be deleted. Click No to cancel the change. Click OK to the message saying that data types were not changed.

8   Change the field size of the Temporary field to Double, with Fixed format and 2 decimal places. Save the table design.

9   Check in datasheet view that all the numbers in the Temporary field are shown with a decimal point followed by two zeros.

10   Change the temporary number for the first Introduction to MS Word course to 123456.65. Also change the temporary number for the second Introduction to MS Word course to 11.25.

11   In design view, change the field size to Single. Save the table design.

Remember:

It is safe to make field sizes bigger in Access. If you make field sizes smaller, you could lose data. Number field sizes, smallest first, are: Byte, Integer, Long Integer, Single, Double.
If you use a different database application instead of Access, it may not always be safe to make fields bigger.

Hint:

Field size is set in design view, and it controls the amount of data that can be stored in the field. The column width for displaying data is set in datasheet view. It is completely separate from field size. Changing the field size in design view has no effect on the column width in datasheet view. Column width has to be adjusted separately.

12 Single is a smaller field size than Double. You should see an error message saying 'Some data may be lost'. Click Yes.

13 In datasheet view, you should find that 123456.65 has changed to 123456.70, but 11.25 is unchanged. Single cannot store 123456.65 properly. There are too many digits.

14 In design view, change the field size to Long Integer. Save the table design.

15 You should see the 'Some data may be lost' message again. Click Yes.

16 In datasheet view, you should see that 123456.65 has changed to 123457.00, and 11.25 has changed to 11.00. Long Integer cannot store decimal places, so Access has rounded the numbers to the nearest whole number.

17 Try changing back to Double. The decimal places do not come back. They have been lost permanently.

18 You may wish to experiment further with changing field sizes. When you have finished, delete the Temporary field.

Task 2.8 Save and print database structures

Method

1 You have already saved the structure of a database table many times. You can use the toolbar Save button. You can click on the File menu and select Save from the drop down list. You can hold down the Ctrl key and press the s key.

2 To print the structure of a table, start with the table closed and the Courses database window showing.

3 Click on the Tools menu and select Analyse from the drop down list, then select Documenter from the sub-menu.

4 The Documenter window should appear.

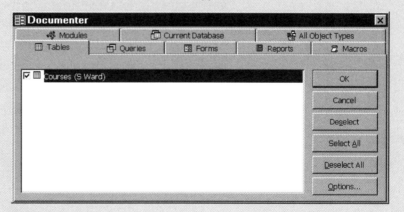

Figure 2.3 Documenter window

Hint:

Instead of the Documenter window, you might see a message, 'Microsoft Access can't start this wizard'. This means that the documenter has not been installed on your computer system. Tell your tutor. If you are at home and have the Microsoft Office installation CDs, you can follow the instructions on the screen and install the documenter.

5 Click in the check box by the name of the Courses table to put in a tick. Click OK.

6 Access examines the structure of the table. This may take a little time. Eventually the Object Definition window appears. There should be about three pages of information about the table, listing each field and giving all its properties.

7 Print out the table structure by clicking the Print button on the toolbar.

8 Close the Object Definition window by clicking the X button in its top right corner.

Information: Copying database tables and table structures

Access lets you copy a table within a database file in three ways. To copy a complete database table, you start with the table closed, but with its name selected in the database window. You can then use the Copy and Paste commands on the table.

- You can copy the entire table, with its structure and data. The copy needs to be given a different name, but otherwise it is exactly the same as the original table. You might want to do this to keep a 'snapshot' of the table as it was at some particular time. You might want to take a copy before making changes to a table, so that you have a temporary backup copy of the table. If the changes go wrong, you can restore the original state of the table.

- You can copy the structure only. The new table has all the same fields as the original, with their data types and properties set as before. There is no data in the new table: it is empty. You can use the new table for a fresh batch of data that you want to keep separate from the data in the original table.

- You can take the data from one table and copy it into another table that has the same structure. For example, you might have one table containing details of customers in Region 1 and another table containing details of customers in Region 2. The regions merge, so you need to combine the two tables. You could copy the contents of one table and **append** (add) them to the other table.

It is also possible to copy a table into a different database file. Again, you start with the table closed, but with its name selected in the database window. Instead of using Copy and Paste, you select the Export command from the File menu.

- You can export the complete table, with its structure and data, into another existing database file.

- You can export the table definition only. This puts an empty table with the same structure as the original table into another existing database file.

- The Export command does not give a method of appending data from one table to a table in another database. There is a method of copying the contents of a table and appending them to an existing table in another database file. This requires an append query. Append queries are covered in Section 5.

Finally, you can open a table or query, select one or more records and use the normal copy and paste commands to copy the records to the end of another table with the same structure.

You will make a new table with the same fields as the Courses table, but the new table will contain no data.

Method

1   Start with the Courses database window on the screen. Select the Courses table name but keep the table closed.
2   Give the Copy command by clicking the Copy button on the toolbar. Nothing seems to happen at this stage, but the table has been copied to the clipboard storage area in the computer's memory.
3   Give the Paste command by clicking the Paste button on the toolbar.
4   A dialogue box should appear, giving you a choice of how you paste the table.

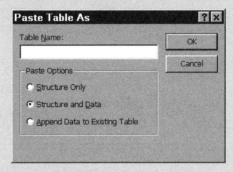

Figure 2.4 Paste Table As dialogue box

5   In the Table Name box, key in a name for the new table: **Full Time Courses**. Add your name in brackets after the table name.
6   Look at the three Paste Options. The first is Structure Only. This will produce a new table with the same fields as the original, but the table will be empty. The second is Structure and Data. This will produce a new table that is the same as the original, containing all the same data. The third option is Append Data to Existing Table. This would take a copy of the data in the Courses table and add the data to the end of another table. We cannot use this option at present because there is no other existing table with the same structure as Courses.
7   Select the Structure Only option by clicking in its round option button.
8   Click OK.
9   Open your new table in datasheet view. It should be empty, but it should have the same field names as the original Courses table.
10 Switch to design view. Change the name of the Sessions field to **Length** and change its data type to **Text** with field size **10**.
11 Save the table structure.
12 Switch to datasheet view and enter the following data:

<table>
<tr><th>Course name</th><th>Site</th><th>Length</th><th>Start date</th><th>Price</th><th>Evening</th></tr>
<tr><td>Intermediate ICT</td><td>main site</td><td>1 year</td><td>07-Sep-02</td><td>£500.00</td><td>No</td></tr>
<tr><td>Advanced ICT</td><td>main site</td><td>2 years</td><td>07-Sep-02</td><td>£900.00</td><td>No</td></tr>
<tr><td>Diploma in IT</td><td>main site</td><td>1 year</td><td>08-Sep-02</td><td>£150.00</td><td>No</td></tr>
</table>

Table 2.4 Data for the Full Time Courses table

13 Close the table.

Hint:

There is no problem with changing field names, data types or field sizes when the table is empty.

Task 2.10 — Copy a complete table, structure and data, within a database file

You will make an exact copy of the Courses table.

Method

1	Starting with the main database window showing the list of tables, select the Courses table but do not open it.
2	Give the Copy command. Nothing seems to happen yet.
3	Give the Paste command so that the Paste Table As dialogue box shows.
4	Key in a name for the new table: **Courses copy (Your name)**. Keep the default option of Structure and Data. Click OK.
5	The new table appears in the list of tables. Open the new table and check that it has the same structure as the Courses table, and contains all the same data.
6	Close the Courses Copy table.

Task 2.11 — Append data from one table to another, within a database file

You can append (add) all the data from one table to the end of another table. Both tables must have the same structure: the same field names and data types. In this task, you will create a new table with the same structure as the Courses table. You will enter data into this new table. You will then append the data from the Courses table to the new table.

Method

1	Starting with the main database window showing the list of tables, select the Courses table but do not open it.
2	Give the Copy command.
3	Give the Paste command so that the Paste Table As dialogue box shows.
4	Give the new table the name **All sites (Your name)**. Select the option to paste Structure Only. Click OK.
5	Open the new All Sites table and enter data as follows:

Course name	Site	Sessions	Start date	Price	Evening
C&G e-Quals Spreadsheet 1	Benfield Centre	15	07-Jan-03	£85.00	No
C&G e-Quals Database 1	Benfield Centre	15	08-Jan-03	£85.00	No
Introducing computers	Ash Ridge School	10	07-Jan-03	£50.00	Yes
Introducing the Internet	Ash Ridge School	10	08-Jan-03	£50.00	Yes

6	Close the table.
7	In the main database window, select the Courses table but do not open it.
8	Give the Copy command.
9	Give the Paste command.
10	In the Paste Table As dialogue box, select the option 'Append Data to Existing Table'. Key in the table name **All sites (Your name)**. Click OK.

11 Open the All Sites table. You should find that all the records from the Courses table have been added to the All Sites table.
12 Close the All Sites table.
13 Close the Courses database by clicking the X button in the top right corner of the database window. This is the window with the title Courses: Database, not the main Microsoft Access window. The Courses database should close, but Access should remain open.

Hint:

You have now used all three ways of copying and pasting a table within a database file. You have pasted structure and data. You have pasted structure only. You have appended data to another table. When you append data, you start by selecting the table that already contains the data. The table name you key into the dialogue box is the table where you want the data to be pasted.

Task 2.12 — Export a complete table to a different database file

You will create a new database file, and copy your existing Courses table (structure and data) from your Courses database into the new database file.

Method

1 Create a new Access database and save it with the name **More Courses**. Close this new database. It does not contain any tables at present.
2 Open your Courses database.
3 Select your Courses table in the database window, but do not open the table.
4 Click on the File menu and select Export from the drop down list.
5 The Export Table dialogue box appears. It looks similar to the Save As dialogue. At the bottom of the window is a box labelled 'Save as type'. Click to show the drop down list, and select Microsoft Access if it is not already selected. Use the dialogue box to find and select your More Courses database. Click the Save button.
6 The Export dialogue box appears.

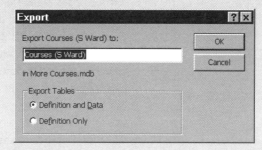

Figure 2.5 The Export dialogue box

7 You could change the name of the table by keying in a new name in the white text box. This time, leave the table name unchanged.
8 You have a choice of exporting the Definition and Data or the Definition Only. This time, keep the default option of Definition and Data. Click OK.
9 A copy of the table has been placed in the More Courses database, but this does not show on the screen because you are still looking at the Courses database.

Hint:

You need to have a table selected, or the Export option on the File menu will be 'greyed out' and not available.

Task 2.13 | Export a table structure to a different database file

You will copy the structure of the Courses table, but not the contents, into a second table in the new database file.

Method

1 Your Courses table should still be selected in the database window.
2 Click on the File menu and select Export from the drop down list.
3 The Export Table dialogue box appears. Find and select your More Courses database. Click the Save button.
4 The Export dialogue box appears.
5 Change the table name to **ExtraCourses** and add your name in brackets. Select Definition Only. Click OK.

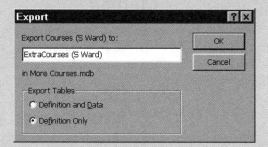

Figure 2.6 Export dialogue box for Definition Only

6 The structure of the Courses table is copied to the More Courses database and given the name ExtraCourses. The contents are not copied, so the ExtraCourses table is empty. You cannot see this yet because you are still looking at the Courses database.
7 Close the Courses database.
8 Open the More Courses database.
9 Check that the database contains two tables. The Courses table should be exactly the same as the original Courses table. The ExtraCourses table should have the same structure, but it should be empty. (There may be default values showing in the first record, but there are no complete records.)
10 Close the More Courses database.

This would be a good point to pause and look back at what you have done. In Task 2.9 you copied the structure of a table to a new table in the same database using a copy and paste method. In Task 2.13 you copied the structure (definition) of the table to a new table in a different database. To do this you used the export method.

In Task 2.10 you copied an entire table, structure and data to a new table in the same database using a copy and paste method. In Task 2.12 you copied an entire table, structure (definition) and data to a new table in a different database using the export method.

Task 2.14 Copy and paste records from one table to another

You will use normal copy and paste methods to copy records from one table to another.

Method

1 Open your Courses database.
2 Open the Courses table.
3 Select the first three records. To do this, you point the mouse to the grey area just to the left of the first record, hold down the left mouse button, and drag the mouse down to point to the left of the third record. All three records should be highlighted with a black background.

Courses (S Ward) : Table			
Course name	Site	Sessions	Start date
Starting MS Word	Community Centre	10	24-Sep-02
Starting MS Word	Riverside	11	25-Sep-02
Starting MS Excel	Community Centre	11	23-Sep-02
Starting Publisher	Riverside	10	23-Sep-02
Using Publisher	Riverside	15	09-Sep-02
MS Word at Work	Riverside	20	11-Sep-02
MS Word Expert	Riverside	4	11-Oct-02
MS Excel Expert	Riverside	4	14-Oct-02

Figure 2.7 Three selected records

Hint:

You must select a complete row before you paste, or the command will not work.

4 Give the Copy command by clicking the Copy button on the toolbar or by any other method you prefer.
5 Close the Courses database.
6 Open the More Courses database and open the Extra Courses table.
7 The Extra Courses table should have no data in it yet. Click on the grey area just to the left of the empty record so that the record is selected with a black background.
8 Give the Paste command by clicking the Paste button on the toolbar or by any other method.
9 Your three records should appear in the table. On most versions of Access a message appears saying, 'You are about to paste 3 record(s). Are you sure you want to paste these records?' Click Yes.
10 Click in any of the records to remove the black background.
11 Close the table and close down Access.

Hint:

Access provides a more flexible method of copying records, called an append query. You will learn to use append queries later.

→ Practise your skills 2.1: Books database

You are asked to make some changes to the database you created in Section 1 to hold records of books for sale in a bookshop.

1 Start Access and open your Books database.

2 Open the Books table in datasheet view.

3 Add the following record:

Stock No	Author	Title	Price	Year_Published	Hardback
34	Colin Dexter	Death is now my neighbour	£9.99	1996	No

Table 2.5 New record for the Books table

4 Change the price of Robinson Crusoe from £15.00 to £14.50.

5 In design view, add a new field called **In Stock** between Price and Year Published. The new field should be a logical field with the Yes/No data type.

6 Enter data into the new field as follows:

Stock No	Author	Title	Price	In Stock
21	Jane Austen	Emma	£2.50	Yes
22	Kazuo Ishiguro	The Unconsoled	£7.99	Yes
23	Miss Read	Life at Thrush Green	£9.99	No
24	Louis de Bernieres	Captain Corelli's Mandolin	£6.99	Yes
25	Vikram Seth	A Suitable Boy	£15.99	Yes
26	Jane Austen	Pride and Prejudice	£2.99	Yes
27	Charles Dickens	Oliver Twist	£18.00	No
28	Daniel Defoe	Robinson Crusoe	£14.50	No
29	Jane Austen	Sense and Sensibility	£2.50	Yes
30	Jane Austen	Persuasion	£2.50	No
31	Kazuo Ishiguro	The Remains of the Day	£6.99	Yes
32	Charles Dickens	David Copperfield	£18.00	Yes
33	Charles Dickens	The Pickwick Papers	£17.00	Yes
34	Colin Dexter	Death is now my neighbour	£9.99	Yes

Table 2.6 Data for the In Stock field

7 In design view, delete the Hardback field.

8 Save and close the table, keeping the Books database open.

9 Make a copy of the Books table, structure and data. Give the new table the name **Books (date)**. Put today's date in the brackets. This copy of the table can be kept to show the state of the table today.

10 Open the new table in datasheet view and check that its contents are the same as the contents of the original Books table. Close the table.

11 Open the original Books table in design view.

12 The stock number system has been changed so that letters may be included in future, e.g. 34a. Change the data type of the Stock No field to Text with a field size of 4. Save the table design.

13 Check in datasheet view that the conversion has been successful and that the stock numbers are shown correctly.

14 In design view, change the field size of the Title field to 40.

15 Change the field size of the Year Published field to Integer. You are making the field size smaller, but there should be no problem because all the numbers in the field are small enough to be stored as Integer. Save the table design.

16 Check in datasheet view that all entries are still displayed correctly.

17 Use Find and Replace to change the author's name **Charles Dickens** to **C Dickens** every time it occurs. Do not put a full stop after the C because this would cause problems later.

18 Print the contents of the Books table on one sheet of paper.

19 Use the documenter to print out the structure of the Books table. There are likely to be three sheets of paper printed.

20 Copy the Books table, structure only, to a new table called **Non Fiction**.

21 Enter the following data into the Non Fiction table:

Stock No	Author	Title	Price	In Stock	Year_Published
87nf	Harold Leighton	Haircutting for Everyone	£15.00	No	1983
88nf	Mark Honan	Austria	£10.99	Yes	1999

Table 2.7 Data for the Non Fiction table

22 Close the table.

23 Append the records from the Non Fiction table to the end of the Books table.

24 Print the Books table again, on one sheet of paper.

25 Delete the two records that you appended in step 23.

You are next asked to create a separate database for use in the Cardiff branch of the bookshop. They need a table with the same structure as the original Books table.

26 Create a new Access database and save it with the name **Cardiff Books**. Close this database.

27 Export the structure (definition) of the Books table from the Books database to the Cardiff Books database. Keep the same table name.

28 Check that the Cardiff Books database now contains an empty Books table.

29 Copy the record for Robinson Crusoe by Daniel Defoe from the Books table of the Books database. Paste the record into the Books table of the Cardiff Books database.

30 Close down Access.

→ Practise your skills 2.2: Seeds database

1 Start Access and open your Seeds database.

2 Open the Seeds table in datasheet view.

3 Add the following record:

CatNo	Name	Price	Available	Type	Height (cm)
AX0297	Snapdragon Kim	£1.99	Yes	HHA	30

Table 2.8 New record for the Seeds table

4 Aster Pink Fizz is no longer available. Make the required change in the Available field.

5 In design view, add a new field called **Start Flowering** between Price and Available. The new field should have the Date/Time data type, formatted to display Short Date.

6 Enter data into the new field as follows:

CatNo	Name	Price	Start Flowering
AX0293	Alyssum	£1.29	01/06/03
AX0298	Snapdragon Delice	£1.99	01/06/03
AX0299	Snapdragon Hobbit	£2.49	01/06/03
AX0320	Aquilegia Winky	£2.99	01/05/03
AX0321	Aquilegia Petticoats	£1.99	01/05/03
AX0334	Aster Pink Fizz	£1.49	01/05/03
AX0335	Aster Blue Magic	£0.99	01/07/03
AX0336	Aster Pink Magic	£0.99	01/07/03
AX0297	Snapdragon Kim	£1.99	01/06/03

Table 2.9 Data for the Start Flowering field

7 In design view, delete the Type field.

8 Save and close the table, keeping the Seeds database open.

9 Make a copy of the Seeds table, structure and data. Give the new table the name **Seeds (version 1 Your name)**.

10 Open the new table in datasheet view and check that its contents are the same as the contents of the original Seeds table. Close the table.

11 Open the original Seeds table in design view.

12 Change the field size of the Height (cm) field from Long Integer to Double. Change the format to Fixed and the number of decimal places to 1.

13 Check in datasheet view that the conversion has been successful and that the heights are shown correctly.

14 In design view, change the field size of the CatNo field to 10. There will be a warning when you save, because you are making the field smaller.

15 Check in datasheet view that all entries are still displayed correctly.

16 Use Find and Replace to change the £1.99 prices to £2.05. There should be three replacements.

17 Print the contents of the table on one sheet of paper.

18 Use the documenter to print out the structure of the Seeds table. There are likely to be three sheets of paper printed. →

19 Copy the Seeds table, structure only, to a new table called **Vegetables**.

20 In the Vegetables table, change the name of the Start Flowering field to **Start Cropping**.

21 Enter the following data into the Vegetables table:

CatNo	Name	Price	Start Cropping	Available	Height (cm)
BX121	Broad Bean Aquadulce	£1.65	01/06/03	Yes	40.00
BX133	French Bean Blue Lake	£1.99	01/08/03	Yes	150.00

Table 2.10 Data for the Vegetables table

22 Close the table and close down Access.

→ Check your knowledge

1 Before using Find and Replace in an Access table, is it necessary to select the field you want to search?

2 Is it safe to make field sizes larger in Access?

3 Is it safe to make field sizes smaller in Access?

4 Can you change a data type from Number to Text without losing data?

5 Can you change from Text to Logical (Yes/No) data type without losing data?

6 You have a database called South Region. This contains a table called Customers. You want an exact copy of this table, in the same database, called CustomersOctober. How would you create this copy?

7 You have a database called South Region. This contains a table called Customers. You want a second database called North Region, containing a table with the same structure as the Customers table, but you want the table to be empty so that you can enter new data. What would you do?

8 How could you copy one of your customer records from the South Region database to the North Region database?

9 You change the field size of a Text field from 20 to 30. What effect does this have on the column width in datasheet view?

10 A table contains a Date/Time field storing dates. You change the data type to Number, then you change it back to Date/Time. Will you lose data?

Section 3 | Keys, indexes and sorting

You will learn to

- Explain the term 'primary key'
- Define a primary key for a table
- Remove a primary key from a table
- Sort records in a table
- Add records to a sorted table
- Create an index on one field
- Create an index on more than one field
- Add records to an indexed table
- Identify the advantages of indexing databases
- Set required and default properties of a field
- Describe the impact of design on the database function

Information: Primary key

A primary key field is used to identify each record uniquely. The field must have a different entry in each record. Consider the Courses table.

Course name	Site	Sessions	Start date	Price	Evening
Starting MS Word	Community Centre	10	24-Sep-02	£50.00	Yes
Starting MS Word	Riverside	11	25-Sep-02	£50.00	No
Starting MS Excel	Community Centre	11	23-Sep-02	£55.00	No
Starting Publisher	Riverside	10	23-Sep-02	£60.00	Yes
Using Publisher	Riverside	15	09-Sep-02	£65.00	Yes
MS Word at Work	Riverside	20	11-Sep-02	£70.00	Yes
MS Word Expert	Riverside	4	11-Oct-02	£80.00	No
MS Excel Expert	Riverside	4	14-Oct-02	£80.00	No

Table 3.1 The Courses table

Could Course name be used as a primary key? No. Two of the records have the same course name. Look at each of the other fields in turn. They all contain duplicate data so none of them is suitable as a primary key. It is not enough just to consider the data in the table at the moment. If it is possible for any field to contain duplicate data then that field will not do as a primary key.

If we want a primary key for the Courses table, then we must create another field that is certain to have a different entry in every record. The usual solution is to give each course a course code or identifier that is unique for that course.

Unique identifiers or codes are commonly used in everyday life. Each person of working age has a National Insurance number. Each bank account has a number. Each item in a catalogue has a catalogue number. Each car has a registration number. Each published book has an ISBN number. These identifiers are likely to make suitable primary keys for tables.

Primary keys are useful in large tables and they are necessary when tables are linked together. If a table has no suitable primary key field then an extra identifier field can be added. Access offers to create an extra field for you when you save a table without a primary key. You have been saying No to this offer. In future you will be setting your own primary key when you create a new table. It is better to set the primary key yourself than to let Access do it for you.

Task 3.1 Define a primary key for a table

You will define a primary key for your Courses table.

Method

1 Open your Courses database, and open your Courses table in design view.
2 There is no existing field that would make a suitable primary key, so create a new field before Course name. Call the new field **Course code**.
3 Give the Course code field the Text data type with a field size of 10. Save the table design.
4 Switch to datasheet view and enter the following data in the Course code field:

Course code	Course name	Site
C211	Starting MS Word	Community Centre
C211a	Starting MS Word	Riverside
C212	Starting MS Excel	Community Centre
C213	Starting Publisher	Riverside
C413	Using Publisher	Riverside
C411	MS Word at Work	Riverside
C611	MS Word Expert	Riverside
C612	MS Excel Expert	Riverside

Table 3.2 Data for the Course code field

Hint:

A primary key field must have a different entry in each record. Each record must have an entry in its primary key field. The Course code field in your table should have a different entry for each record. Every record must have an entry in the Course code field. If there is an error message when you try to save the table design, then remove the primary key (see Task 3.2). Check in datasheet view that there are no duplicate course codes and no empty records apart from one 'new' record marked with an asterisk (*). Correct any course codes and delete any empty records. Try defining the primary key again.

5 Switch back to design view. Make sure that the Course code field is selected. Click the Primary Key button on the toolbar. It looks like a little yellow key 🔑
6 A key should appear in the left margin next to the Course code field name.

Figure 3.1 Course code set as a primary key field

7 Look at the properties of the Course code field in the lower part of the window. The Indexed property should be set to Yes (No Duplicates).
8 Save the table design.
9 Switch to datasheet view and change the Course code for Using Publisher to C213. Try to click out of the record into a different record. There should be an error message warning you that you cannot have duplicate values in a primary key. Click OK. Change the Course code back to C413. You should now be able to click out of the record.

Method

I	In design view, select the Course code field.
2	Click the Primary Key button on the toolbar to remove the key from the margin beside the field name. Course code is no longer the primary key for the table.
3	Look at the field properties. The Indexed property should now say 'Yes (Duplicates OK)'.
4	Save the table design.

Information: Sorting records

It is very common for the user of a database to want to sort the records for display or printing. Access provides a variety of sorting facilities. You can sort records quickly in a table, but the sorting is not saved. You can save a sorted order of records using a query. You will see later that you can also sort records for printing in a report. Here we shall sort records in a table.

You may be asked to add a record to a sorted table. Access will not let you insert the new record into its sorted position in the table. Instead you add all new records at the end of the table. You can then sort the table again so that the new records go to their sorted positions.

Number fields, currency fields and date fields are sorted by their values, either ascending (smallest or earliest first) or descending (largest C or latest first). Text fields are sorted alphabetically, either ascending (A to Z) or descending (Z to A). Numbers stored in text fields (e.g. phone numbers or reference numbers) are not sorted by the value of the number, but by taking each digit in turn and treating it as a character.

Sorted in a number field: 1, 2, 3, 10, 12, 21, 25, 33, 100
Sorted in a text field: 1, 10, 100, 12, 2, 21, 25, 3, 33.

Method

I	Switch to datasheet view of the Courses table.
2	Click into the Start date field.
3	Click the Sort Ascending button on the toolbar A/Z↓. The records should be sorted in ascending order of start date with the earliest date first and the latest date last.
4	Click into the Price field.
5	Click the Sort Descending button on the toolbar Z/A↓. The records should be sorted by price, with the most expensive course first.

Method

1   Add the following records to the end of the table:

Course code	Course name	Site	Sessions	Start date	Price	Evening
C216	Starting MS Access	Riverside	11	25-Sep-02	£55.00	True
C416	MS Access at Work	Riverside	20	11-Sep-02	£75.00	True
C616	MS Access Expert	Riverside	4	15-Oct-02	£85.00	True

Table 3.3 New records for the Courses table

2   Click into the Price field and click the Sort Descending button on the toolbar.
3   Check that the new records are now in their sorted positions.

Information: Indexes and their advantages

An index in a book lets you find topics quickly. An index in a database table has a similar purpose. It speeds up searching and sorting on a field. In your City & Guilds work you have been using very small databases so that sorting and searching are very quick. Commercial databases are generally very large. There may be many thousands of records. Sorting and searching could take a long time. Indexing a field can make a big improvement in the speed of sorting or searching on that field. Adding an index increases the size of the database a little, but it is usually worthwhile for the improvement in performance. Saving the database tends to be slowed down a little if there is an index, but the faster sorting and searching usually more than makes up for this.

It is usually good design to put an index on any field that is likely to be used for sorting or searching. Primary key fields are always automatically indexed. You could index all the fields in a table, but this is not usually necessary or sensible. Remember that indexes do increase the size of the database a bit, and they slow down the saving process.

Another advantage of indexes is that you can create an index on more than one field. You can then sort on both fields together. Sorting on more than one field is very useful where the main sorting field has the same entry in several records. Think of the phone book. It sorts people by their surnames. Some surnames are quite common, and shared by a large number of people. The phone book does a second sort on initials so that people with the same surname are sorted by their initials. Surname is the primary sort field and Initials is the secondary sort field. Do not confuse a primary sort field with a primary key. Primary sort field just means that you sort on that field first.

Task 3.5 — Create an index on one field

You will create a primary key again, then you will create two more indexes.

Method

1 In design view of the Courses table, select the Course code field and click the Primary Key button on the toolbar to make Course code the primary key.

2 Select the Course name field. Look at its Indexed property in the lower part of the window. The Indexed property should be set to No.

3 Click into the Indexed property box. An arrow should appear at the right of the box. Click the arrow to show the drop down list.

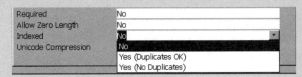

Figure 3.2 The Indexed property of a field

4 Select Yes (Duplicates OK) from the list. This creates an index on the field. Course name is not a primary key, so duplicate values are allowed.

5 Click the Indexes button on the toolbar ![icon]. This displays a window with a list of existing indexes.

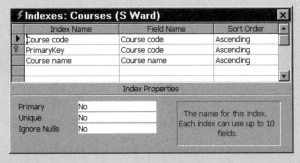

Figure 3.3 The Indexes window

6 In the Indexes window, you can see that the Course code has two indexes. One is an ordinary index called Course code. The other is a special index called PrimaryKey. (You may have only the Primary Key index on Course code. It depends on how the options have been set in your version of Access.) The Course name field has an index called Course name.

7 You can use the Indexes dialogue box to create new indexes. First you will create an index on the Start date field. Each index needs a name. Click into the Index Name column in the first empty row. Key in **Start**. The index name does not have to be the same as the name of the field.

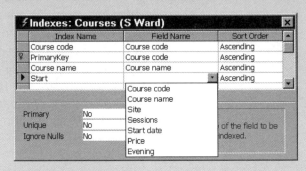

Figure 3.4 Creating an index using the Indexes window

Hint:

To set an index on a single field, you can either use the field properties at the bottom of the design window or you can use the Indexes window.

To remove an index you can either use the field properties and change the Indexed property to No, or you can delete the index from the Indexes window.

Hint:

You may find that Access indexes some fields for you automatically. The Course code field had two indexes. You created one when you made Course code the primary key. Access created the other. Access is set up by default to look for field names containing text such as 'code', 'ID', 'num' or 'key', and automatically index fields with such names.

Automatic indexing is an option that can be changed, and your version of Access may not be set up to do it.

8	Tab or click into the Field Name column. An arrow should appear. Click the arrow to see the drop down list.
9	Select Start date from the drop down list of field names. Leave the sort order as ascending.
10	Close the Indexes window by clicking the X button in its top right corner.
11	Select the Start date field and look at its properties. The Indexes property should now be Yes (Duplicates OK).
12	Save the table structure.

Task 3.6 Create an index on more than one field

You will create an index to sort first on the Site field and then on the Sessions field.

Method

1   Click the Indexes button on the toolbar to show the Indexes window.
2   Key in a new index name: **SiteSessions**.
3   Click into the Field Name column in the same row and select Site from the drop down list.
4   Move down to Field Name column in the next row and select Sessions from the drop down list. It is important to leave the Index Name box empty in the Sessions row.

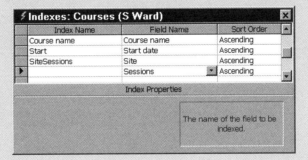

Figure 3.5 An index on two fields

5   You now have an index called SiteSessions that will sort first on the Site field and second on the Sessions field. Close the Indexes window.
6   Save the table design.
7   Switch to datasheet view.
8   Select the Site field and click the Sort Ascending button on the toolbar.
9   Check that the table has been sorted first by site, with Community Centre coming before Riverside. Within site, it should be sorted by the number of sessions.

Course code	Course name	Site	Sessions	Start date	Price	Evening
C211	Starting MS Word	Community Centre	10	24-Sep-02	£50.00	Yes
C212	Starting MS Excel	Community Centre	11	23-Sep-02	£55.00	No
C611	MS Word Expert	Riverside	4	11-Oct-02	£80.00	No
C612	MS Excel Expert	Riverside	4	14-Oct-02	£80.00	No
C616	MS Access Expert	Riverside	4	15-Oct-02	£85.00	Yes
C213	Starting Publisher	Riverside	10	23-Sep-02	£60.00	Yes
C211a	Starting MS Word	Riverside	11	25-Sep-02	£50.00	No
C216	Starting MS Access	Riverside	11	25-Sep-02	£55.00	Yes
C413	Using Publisher	Riverside	15	09-Sep-02	£65.00	Yes
C411	MS Word at Work	Riverside	20	11-Sep-02	£70.00	Yes
C416	MS Access at Work	Riverside	20	11-Sep-02	£75.00	Yes

Table 3.4 The Courses table sorted by Site then by Sessions

Hint:

Setting an index does not automatically sort a table. In many cases you will still have to select the field and click the Sort button. In a small database you will not find that an index on a single field makes any difference to the sorting. The advantage comes when the database is large. If there is an index on two or more fields, you only need to sort the first field. The other fields will automatically be sorted within the first sort. You did not need to sort on Sessions. The field was sorted automatically within the Site sort.

Task 3.7 — Add records to an indexed table

Method

1 Add the following records to the end of the Courses table:

Course code	Course name	Site	Sessions	Start date	Price	Evening
C219	Introducing the Internet	Community Centre	12	25-Sep-02	£50.00	Yes
C419	Creating a web page	Riverside	12	25-Sep-02	£65.00	Yes

Table 3.5 New records for the Courses table

2 Select the Site field and click the Sort Ascending button on the toolbar. The records should be sorted into their correct places.

Task 3.8 — Set required and default properties of a field

Method

1. In design view, select the Course name field.
2. Look at the field properties in the lower part of the window. The Required property shows **No**. This means that you do not have to enter a course name in a record. You could leave the field empty. It is probably not a good idea to leave the course name field empty, and you can force the database user to enter something in the field by setting the Required property to Yes.
3. Click into the Required property box, so that an arrow appears. Click the arrow to show the drop down list and select Yes.
4. Save the table structure. You should see a warning message starting 'Data integrity rules have been changed...'. It offers to check that the existing data meets the new rules. Click Yes to run the check. Access will check that there are no records with an empty course name field.
5. In datasheet view, delete the course name Using Publisher, leaving the field empty. Try to move to another record. There should be an error message saying that you must enter data in the field. Key in Using Publisher again or use the Undo button on the toolbar to undo the deletion. Now you should be able to move to another record.
6. In design view, select the Site field. Find the Default property in the lower part of the design window. Key in a default value: **Riverside**.
7. Save the table design.
8. In datasheet view, look at the bottom row of the table which is ready for a new record to be entered. The Site field already contains the default entry, Riverside. Since Riverside is the most common entry in this field, it saves time to have it already entered. The database user can replace it with a different entry if necessary. Notice that number fields automatically have a default entry of 0.
9. Close the Courses table and close down Access. Answer Yes if you are asked to save changes.

Hint:

When changing the Required property from No to Yes, instead of showing the drop down list and selecting, you can double click on **No** to change it to **Yes**.

Hint:

Database users can be confused and upset if they find that they are unable to click out of a record or do anything at all as long as a Required field is empty. Use the Required property only when it is really needed. You should provide detailed instructions for the user explaining that there must be an entry in the field, and telling them what will happen if they do not make the entry.

Information: The impact of design on the database function

A database can be developed into a complex application with many facilities for searching, sorting, display and printing. In order for all these facilities to work properly, the basics of the database must be right. That means that the table or tables must be designed well. The fields, their data types and their properties must be chosen to store and retrieve the data efficiently.

Some aspects of design are:
- A field should contain the smallest item of data that is likely to be of interest. It is usual to split a person's name into surname and forename fields so that the surname can be handled separately for sorting and searching. It is usual to split an address into several fields so that the postal town and the postcode have their own fields.

- A table should generally store records with details of only one kind of person or thing: Customers, Employees, Books for sale, Training courses offered, Computer equipment in the offices. Each of these needs a separate table.
- Fields should be indexed if they are likely to be used for sorting or searching.
- Other field properties, such as Required and Default, can be used to help database users to enter data correctly.

There are other design features that become important when you link tables to create a relational database. In every case, the database must be suitable for its purpose. The designer must find out exactly what is needed before starting the database design.

→ Practise your skills 3.1: Books database

1 Open your Books database and open the Books table in design view.

2 Make **Stock No** the primary key of the table.

3 Create an index on the Author field. Save the table design.

4 Give the In Stock field a default value of **Yes**.

5 Make the Author and Title fields required.

6 In datasheet view, sort the records alphabetically in ascending order by Author. (Note that the sorting is by first name. The table has not been designed for sorting by surname.)

7 Add the following records and print the table showing these new records in their sorted order. (You will need to sort again before printing.)

Stock No	Author	Title	Price	In Stock	Year_Published
35	Colin Dexter	The Dead of Jericho	£9.99	No	1996
36	Daniel Defoe	Robinson Crusoe	£5.99	Yes	1999
37	John Galsworthy	The Forsyte Saga	£9.50	Yes	2002

Table 3.6 Three new records for the Books table

8 Create an index on the Price field, then sort the records in ascending order of Price.

9 Add the following records and print the table sorted in order of Price.

Stock No	Author	Title	Price	In Stock	Year_Published
38	D H Lawrence	Sons and Lovers	£2.99	No	1999
39	John Le Carre	Tinker Tailor Soldier Spy	£5.30	No	1996

Table 3.7 Two new records for the Books table

10 Create an index called **AuthorTitle** to sort first on the Author field and second on the Title field.

11 Sort the table by Author, and by Title within Author. (Just sort by Author and the index will automatically do the second sort by Title.)

12 Add the following record and print the table in its new sorted order.

Stock No	Author	Title	Price	In Stock	Year_Published
40	John Le Carre	Call for the Dead	£5.30	Yes	1996

Table 3.8 One new record for the Books table

13 Delete the index on the Price field. (Change its Indexed property to No.)

14 Close your Books table and close down Access. Save any changes if you are prompted to do so.

→ Practise your skills 3.2: Seeds database

1 Open your Seeds database and open the Seeds table.

2 Make the CatNo field the primary key of the Seeds table.

3 Create an index on the Height field.

4 Sort the records in order of Height.

5 Add the following record, then print out all the records in their sorted order. (You will need to sort again after adding the record.)

CatNo	Name	Price	Start Flowering	Available	Height (cm)
AX0342	Dahlia Minstrel Mixture	£1.65	01/07/03	No	30.00

Table 3.9 One new record for the Seeds table

6 Make the Name field required.

7 Give the Start Flowering field a default value of 01/07/03 and give the Available field a default value of Yes.

8 Create an index called **DateName** that will sort first by Start Flowering and second by Name.

9 Sort the records by the Start Flowering date, and by Name within Start Flowering.

10 Add the following records, then print all the records in their sorted order.

CatNo	Name	Price	Start Flowering	Available	Height (cm)
AX0343	Dahlia Rigoletto	£1.99	01/07/03	Yes	38.00
AX0356	Ipomoea Cardinal	£1.19	01/07/03	Yes	300.00
AX0360	Lupin Gallery Mixed	£2.25	01/06/03	Yes	50.00

Table 3.10 Three new records for the Seeds table

11 Delete the index on the Height field.

12 Close the table and close down Access.

→ Check your knowledge

1 Which of the following fields is likely to be the most suitable primary key for a table of Employees?
- Surname
- Forename
- Job Title
- Payroll number
- Department

2 What is the main purpose of indexing a field?

3 Why are you not likely to notice much benefit from indexing fields in the tables you create for your City & Guilds work?

4 Why should you not index every field?

5 If you sort an Employees table with Department as the primary sort field and Surname as the secondary sort field, what will happen?

6 Is a primary key always indexed in Access?

7 Is every indexed field a primary key?

8 If you create an index on a field in Access, does that automatically sort the table?

9 What is the effect of setting the Required property of a field to Yes?

10 The Employees table has a Department field. What is the effect of setting the Default property of a Department field to Accounts?

You are asked to create a database to store records of customers of a mail order business. The database should store the name and address of each customer, the value and date of the most recent order, whether or not the customer should get a discount on the next order, and a unique account number for each customer.

1 Create a new Access database called **Customers**.
2 Create a table with the following structure:

Field name	Data type	Field size/format
Title	Text	10
Initials	Text	10
Surname	Text	30
Street	Text	30
Town	Text	50
County	Text	30
Postcode	Text	10
Date	Date/Time	Short date
Value	Number	Long Integer
Discount	Yes/No	Yes/No
AccNo	Number	Long Integer

Table 3.11 Structure of the Customers table

3 Make AccNo the primary key field for the table.
4 Create an index on the Value field, allowing duplicates.
5 The Postcode field should have an index. You may find that Access has already indexed the Postcode field. Access may be set up to index all fields with names containing certain text such as 'code', 'num' and 'ID'.
6 Create an index called FullName that will sort first on Surname and then on Initials.
7 Make the Surname and Postcode fields Required.
8 Give the County field a default value of **Oxon**.
9 Save the table with the name **Customers**.
10 Enter the following data:

Title	Initials	Surname	Street	Town	County	Postcode	Date	Value	Discount	AccNo
Mr	P	Schwartz	12 Wayne Drive	Abingdon	Oxon	OX14 1JD	13/06/02	250	Yes	1
Ms	F	Maybee	15 Curzon Lane	Witney	Oxon	OX28 4GH	06/02/02	105	No	2
Dr	N B	Thoms	21 Neil Close	Abingdon	Oxon	OX14 2BN	15/03/02	305	Yes	3
Mrs	D	Jarvis	11 Green Road	Radley Abingdon	Oxon	OX14 3SM	14/12/01	87	No	4
Mr	V	Singh	6 Broom Close	Didcot	Oxon	OX11 7HW	03/07/01	32	No	5
Mr	S H	Lacon	8 Norton Street	Oxford	Oxon	OX3 7BW	04/08/01	220	Yes	6
Ms	C	Perkins	52 Orly Avenue	Earley Reading	Berks	RG6 3BL	03/05/02	450	Yes	7
Miss	M	Golding	6 High Street	Didcot	Oxon	OX11 8DU	12/11/00	98	No	8
Mr	S	Way	9 Station Road	Earley Reading	Berks	RG6 5PS	20/05/02	207	Yes	9
Ms	R B	Adams	3 Kenton Road	Abingdon	Oxon	OX14 3NM	30/03/02	39	No	10
Ms	N	Quilling	32 Park Place	Reading	Berks	RG3 9SK	28/07/02	500	Yes	11
Dr	L	Smith	42 Acton Lane	Earley Reading	Berks	RG6 2JV	30/03/02	205	Yes	12
Mr	A	Hussein	2 Carters Close	Oxford	Oxon	OX2 2HH	19/04/02	350	Yes	13
Mr	N	Jarvis	11 Green Road	Radley Abingdon	Oxon	OX14 3SM	25/02/02	175	No	14

Table 3.12 Data for the Customers table

11 Copy the whole table, data and structure, to a new table called **Area3**.

12 Copy the structure only of the Customers table to a new table called **Area6**.

13 In the Area6 table, change the default value of the County field to **Devon**.

14 Enter the following data into the Area6 table.

Title	Initials	Surname	Street	Town	County	Postcode	Date	Value	Discount	AccNo
Mr	N	Smith	12 South Street	Torquay	Devon	TQ1 4NN	03/05/02	50	No	100
Ms	K G	Grant	1 Palm Drive	Torquay	Devon	TQ2 1GN	11/12/01	360	Yes	101
Ms	H	Smith	43 Anstee Close	Paignton	Devon	TQ4 7DM	06/06/02	87	No	102
Mr	N	Hussein	6 Conway Close	Torquay	Devon	TQ2 9DD	15/06/02	205	Yes	103
Ms	K	Adams	2 Green Road	Paignton	Devon	TQ4 6BL	19/01/02	152	Yes	104

Table 3.13 Data for the Area6 table

15 Copy the data from the Area6 table into the Customers table. (To do this, close the Area6 table. Copy and paste the Area6 table, select Append Data to Existing Table, then key in Customers as the table name and click OK.)

16 Open the Customers table and check that it contains the records for Area 3 and for Area 6.

17 Use your FullName index to sort the records in ascending order of Surname and Initials within Surname. Check that the sorting is correct. Customers who share the same surname should be sorted in order of initials.

18 Print the Customers table in its sorted order, using landscape orientation.

19 Close the Customers table and the Customers database, but leave Access open.

20 Create a new database and call it **WestCustomers**. (Start with File – New, or click the New button on the toolbar.)

21 Close your new WestCustomers database.

22 Open your Customers database.

23 Export a copy of the structure (definition only) of your Area 6 table to the WestCustomers database, giving the new table the name **DevonCustomers**. (Remember, select the Area 6 table. Then use the File menu and select Export.)

24 Still in your Customers database, open the Area 6 table and sort the records by Town.

25 Select the records of customers who live in Torquay. Copy these records and paste them into the DevonCustomers table of your WestCustomers database.

26 Print out your DevonCustomers table to show the three records.

27 Use the documenter to print out the structure of your DevonCustomers table.

28 Close down Access.

29 Make a backup copy of your Customers.mdb file in your AccessBackup folder. Give the copied file a name that shows it is a backup copy of the Customers database. Also make a backup copy of your WestCustomers database and give it a suitable name.

Section 4 | Select queries

You will learn to

- Describe the use of a query or filter
- Create a query
- Create a query to search on a logical field
- Create a query using a relational operator
- Select dates using between ... and
- Describe the use of logical operators
- Create a query using OR with two criteria on the same field
- Create a query using OR with two criteria on different fields
- Create a query using AND with two criteria on different fields
- Create a query using AND with two criteria on the same field
- Create queries with more than two criteria
- Create a query using a wild card
- Create a query to sort on two fields

Information: Select queries and filters

So far you have been working with database tables. In this section you will use another kind of database object, the **query**. A query does not store any data. It takes the data from one or more tables and processes it. The simplest form of query is the **select query**, used to select and sort records. Selecting records is sometimes called **filtering**. You filter the records, keeping the ones you want and discarding the ones that you do not want.

In order to select or filter records you use one or more criteria. A criterion is a rule that you make for Access to obey when it filters records. For example, to filter records from the Courses table you might use the criterion **Site = Riverside**. Courses on the Riverside site will be selected and the others will not.

Select queries are useful in their own right. They are also important because they can be used as a base for creating other database objects such as reports for printing.

We shall do all our selecting of records using queries. You might like to know that Access provides a facility called a filter in its tables. This can be used to filter records quickly and temporarily, but the selection cannot be saved and the filter in a table is far less powerful than a query. If you are asked to 'filter' records, use a query.

You should always check the results of queries to make sure that the right records have been selected. You will need an up-to-date printout of the complete table to help you check. If you do not have a printout of the table then make one before you start creating queries.

Task 4.1   Create a query

You will select courses on the Riverside site. The method should be familiar from Level 1.

Method

1   Open your Courses database.
2   In the database window, click on the Queries button to show the Queries section of the database.
3   Double click with the mouse on 'Create query in design view'.
4   The query design window appears with the Show Table dialogue box in front of it. Select the Courses table in the dialogue box and click Add.
5   A list of fields in the Courses table should appear in the top section of the query design window. Close the Show Table dialogue box.
6   Add all the fields to the query design grid in the lower half of the window. The quickest way is to double click on the table name so that all the fields are selected, then drag all the fields down and drop them in the left column of the grid.

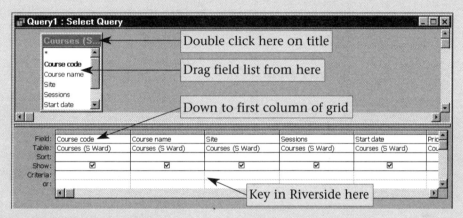

Figure 4.1 Adding all fields to a query design grid

7   Click into the Criteria row of the Site column and key in **Riverside**.
8   Save the query with the name **qryRiverside**.
9   Switch to datasheet view to see the result of the query.
10   Check that the correct records are shown. Then close the query.

Hint:

You can add field names to the query design grid one at a time. Methods include:

1   Drag a single field name to a column of the grid.
2   Double click on a field name and it will go to the first empty column.
3   Click into the Field row of the grid and select a field name from the drop down list that will appear.

Task 4.2   Create a query to search on a logical field

You will show a list of evening classes sorted in order of starting date.

Method

1   Create a new query in design view. Add the Courses table.
2   Put all the fields in the query design grid.
3   Click into the Criteria row of the Evening field. You may need to scroll sideways to find the field. Key in **True**.

4 Click into the Sort row of the Start date field and select Ascending from the drop down list.

Start date	Price	Evening
Courses (S Ward)	Courses (S Ward)	Courses (S Ward)
Ascending		
☑	☑	☑
		True

Figure 4.2 Selecting evening courses sorted by start date

5 Save the query as **qryEvening**.
6 Switch to datasheet view and check that the correct records are displayed and sorted.
7 Close the query.

Information: Relational operators

Relational operators are often used in queries. They should be familiar from Level 1, but here they are again:

equals	=
less than	<
greater than	>
less than or equal to	<=
greater than or equal to	>=
not equal to	<>

Take care with 'less than or equal to' and 'greater than or equal to'. You must put the symbols the right way round or the query will not work.

Task 4.3   Create a query using a relational operator

You will create a query to show courses with 10 or more sessions. Some of the fields will not be shown.

Method

1 Create a new query in design view. Add the Courses table.
2 Put all the fields in the query design grid.
3 Click into the Criteria row of the Sessions field. Key in >=10.
4 Click into the Sort row of the Course code field and select Ascending from the drop down list.
5 Remove the tick from the check box in the Show row of the Site field, the Price field and the Evening field. These fields will not be displayed.

Instead of switching to
datasheet view of a select
query, you can run it by
clicking the Run button on
the toolbar. The button
shows an exclamation
mark. In the case of a
select query, datasheet
view and running the query
have the same effect. This
is not true of other queries
that you will meet later.

Course code	Course name	Site	Sessions
Courses (S Ward)	Courses (S Ward)	Courses (S Ward)	Courses (S Ward)
Ascending			
☑	☑	☐	☑
			>=10

Figure 4.3 Courses with 10 or more sessions

6　Save the query as **qry10ormore**.

7　Switch to datasheet view and check that the correct records and fields are
shown in their sorted order. There should be 10 records and 4 fields.

8　Close the query.

Task 4.4　Select dates using between ... and

You will show courses that start between 23-Sept-02 and 11-Oct-02
inclusive.

Method

1　Create a new query in design view. Add the Courses table.

2　Put all the fields in the query design grid.

3　Click into the criteria row of the Start date field. Key in **Between 23/09/02
And 11/10/02**. Take care to leave a space after 'Between' and before and
after 'And'. Do not include the full stop.

4　Press the Enter key and you should see hash marks # appear round the
dates.

5　Save the query as **qryDatesBetween**.

6　Switch to datasheet view or run the query. Check that the correct records
are shown. There should be eight records.

7　Close the query.

Information: Logical operators

You might need to select records using more than one criterion at a
time. People might ask you: Which courses have 10 or 11 sessions?
Which courses are held at Riverside and cost less than £70? Are there
any evening classes at Riverside in Starting MS Word?

You use the logical operators AND and OR to search on more than one
criterion. If both criteria must be true then you use AND. If it is
enough for one of the criteria to be true then you use OR.

Example:
Starting MS Word is held at Riverside in the daytime. It has 11 sessions
and costs £50.
Site = Riverside is TRUE
Price < £70 is TRUE
Evening is FALSE
Site = Riverside AND Price < £70 is TRUE because both criteria are
true

Site = Riverside AND Evening is FALSE
Site = Riverside OR Price < £70 is TRUE
Site = Riverside OR Evening is TRUE. Only one criterion need be true with OR

If you join criteria in a query by using AND, then you are being stricter in your selection, because you are requiring both criteria to be true. You are likely to have fewer records displayed than if you used one criterion alone.

If you join criteria using OR, then you are being less strict, because you are only requiring one of the criteria to be true. You are likely to have more records displayed than if you used one criterion alone.

There is another logical operator, NOT.
Site = Riverside is TRUE, so
Site = NOT Riverside is FALSE

Task 4.5   Create a query using OR with two criteria on the same field

You will select courses with 10 or 11 sessions.

Method

1	Create a new query in design view. Add the Courses table.		
2	Put all the fields in the query design grid.		
3	Click into the Criteria row of the Sessions field and key in **10**.		
4	Move down into the Or row and key in **11**.		

Field:	Course code	Course name	Site	Sessions
Table:	Courses (S Ward)	Courses (S Ward)	Courses (S Ward)	Courses (S Ward)
Sort:				
Show:	☑	☑	☑	☑
Criteria:				10
or:				11

Figure 4.4 Courses with 10 or 11 sessions

5	Save the query as **qry10or11Sessions**.
6	Switch to datasheet view and check that the right records are shown. There should be 5 courses with 10 or 11 sessions.
7	Close the query. (Do not skip this step. It matters.)
8	Open the query again in design view.
9	Look at the criterion. Access changes it to **10 Or 11** in the Criteria row. You could have keyed in **10 Or 11** yourself. The result would be the same.
10	Close the query.

Task 4.6	Create a query using OR with two criteria on different fields

You will select courses that have more than 12 sessions or cost more than £70.

Method

1   Create a new query in design view. Add the Courses table.
2   Put all the fields in the query design grid.
3   Click into the Criteria row of the Sessions field and key in **>12**.
4   Click in the Or row of the Price field and key in **>70**.

Field:	Course name	Site	Sessions	Start date	Price
Table:	Courses (S Ward)	Courses (S Ward)	Courses (S Ward)	Courses (S Ward)	Courses (S Ward)
Sort:					
Show:	☑	☑	☑	☑	☑
Criteria:			>12		
or:					>70

Figure 4.5 Courses with more than 12 sessions or costing more than £70

5   Save the query as **qrySessionsOrPrice**.
6   Switch to datasheet view and check the result. There should be six records with codes C413, C411, C611, C612, C416, C616. These are the records of courses that either have more than 12 sessions or cost more than £70 or both.
7   Close the query.

Hint:

Do not key in £ signs in criteria. Make sure you use the Or row and not the Criteria row for the Price field.

Task 4.7	Create a query using AND with two criteria on different fields

You will find courses that start on or before 25th September and have 11 sessions.

Method

1   Create a new query in design view. Add the Courses table.
2   Put all the fields in the query design grid.
3   Click into the Criteria row of the Start date field and key in **<=25/09/02**.
4   Click into the Criteria row of the Sessions field and key in **11**. Criteria in the same row are combined using AND.

Field:	Course code	Course name	Site	Sessions	Start date
Table:	Courses (S Ward)	Courses (S Ward)	Courses (S Ward)	Courses (S Ward)	Courses (S Ward)
Sort:					
Show:	☑	☑	☑	☑	☑
Criteria:				11	<=#25/09/02#
or:					

Figure 4.6 Courses with 11 sessions starting on or before 25th September

5   Save the query as **qryDateAndSessions**.
6   Switch to datasheet view and check the result. There should be three courses with codes C211a, C212 and C216.
7   Close the query.

Task 4.8 | Create a query using AND with two criteria on the same field

You will find courses costing more than £60 and less than £80.

Hint:

Courses costing exactly £60 or exactly £80 are not included when you use **>60 And <80**. To include these courses you could use **>=60 And <=80**. Alternatively you could use **Between 60 And 80**.

Method

1   Create a new query in design view. Add the Courses table.
2   Put all the fields in the query design grid.
3   Click into the Criteria row of the Price field and key in **>60 And <80**.

Field:	Site	Sessions	Start date	Price
Table:	Courses (S Ward)	Courses (S Ward)	Courses (S Ward)	Courses (S Ward)
Sort:				
Show:	☑	☑	☑	☑
Criteria:				>60 And <80
or:				

Figure 4.7 Courses costing more than £60 and less than £80

Remember:

Criteria in the same row are combined using AND. Criteria in different rows are combined using OR.

4   Save the query as **qryMorethan60Lessthan80**.
5   Switch to datasheet view and check the result. There should be four courses with codes C413, C411, C416 and C419.
6   Close the query.

Task 4.9 | Create queries with more than two criteria

You will find courses at Riverside that have more than 10 sessions and start before 20 September 2002.

Method

1   Create a new query in design view. Add the Courses table.
2   Put all the fields in the query design grid.
3   Decide what criteria you need and which fields they should go in. Enter all the criteria in the same row, since they must all be true together. They are linked by AND.
4   Save the query as **qryRiversideGr10Bef20Sep**.
5   Switch to datasheet view and check the result. There should be three courses with codes C413, C411 and C416.
6   Close the query.

You will find courses at Riverside that have 10 or 11 sessions.

Method

1 Create a new query in design view. Add the Courses table.
2 Put all the fields in the query design grid.
3 Take care with the criteria for this one.

Field:	Course name	Site	Sessions	Start date
Table:	Courses (S Ward)	Courses (S Ward)	Courses (S Ward)	Courses (S Ward)
Sort:				
Show:	☑	☑	☑	☑
Criteria:		"Riverside"	10	
or:		"Riverside"	11	

Figure 4.8 Courses at Riverside with 10 or 11 sessions

Riverside appears in both rows because we want 10-week courses at Riverside or 11-week courses at Riverside.

4 Save the query as **qryRiverside10or11**.
5 Switch to datasheet view and check the result. There should be three courses with codes C211a, C213 and C216.

Information: Wildcards

Sometimes you may want to search for part of the text in a field and not the whole field. For example, you might want to select course names that contain 'Excel'. You can do this kind of searching using **wildcards**. In card games, a wildcard is a playing card that can be used in place of other playing cards. The same sort of idea applies to wildcards in searching. There are two wildcards used by Access: **?** and *****.

? can be used to stand for any other single character. For example, p?t could stand for pat, pet, pit, pot or put. Ca? could stand for cab, cap, cat, can, and so on.

* can be used to stand for any number of characters, or none at all. For example, p*t could stand for pat, planet, pivot, privet, prettiest, and so on. Ca* could stand for cab, cabinet, cart, capital, calligraphy, and so on.

Hint:

To find course names starting with Excel you would use Excel*. To find course names ending with Excel you would use *Excel. You can make use of spaces. Excel * with a space would find 'Excel for Beginners' but it would not find 'Excellent Yoga Class'. Excel* without the space would find both.

Task 4.10 Create a query using a wildcard

You will find all courses with Excel in the course name.

Method

1 Create a new query in design view. Add the Courses table.
2 Put all the fields in the query design grid.
3 Click into the Criteria row of the Course name field and key in ***Excel***. The wildcard is needed before and after Excel because there might be characters before Excel, after Excel or both.

4 Press the Enter key and notice that the criterion changes to Like "*Excel*".

5 Save the query as **qryExcel**.

6 Switch to datasheet view. There should be two Excel courses listed.

7 Close the query.

Task 4.11   Create a query to sort on two fields

You will sort the courses first by site and then by start date within site.

Method

I Create a new query in design view. Add the Courses table.

2 Put all the fields in the query design grid.

3 Set both the Site field and the Start date field to sort ascending.

4 Save the query as **qrySortSiteDate**.

5 Switch to datasheet view and check that the records are sorted first by site, then by start date within site.

6 Close the query.

Task 4.12   Create a query to sort on two fields displayed in a different order

Remember:

You can sort records on more than one field in a table by setting an index on the fields.

When you set more than one field to sort in a query, the leftmost field is sorted first. Site is to the left of Start date, so Site is sorted first. Suppose that you want to sort on Start date first and then by Site within Start date. You have two options. The first is to put in the fields in a different order so that Start date is to the left of Site. This is fine as long as you want the fields displayed in that order. The other option is to put the Start date field in twice, once on the left of Site and once on the right. Sort on the leftmost Start date field, but hide it. The second Start date field shows but is not sorted. You then have the sort you want, but the fields are still displayed in the right order.

Method

I Create a new query in design view. Add the Courses table.

2 Put all the fields in the query design grid.

3 Add the Start date field again, on the left of the Site field. To do this, point the mouse to the Start date field in the list of field names in the upper part of the window. Drag the Start date field name down and drop it on top of the Site field name in the query design grid. The Site field and the other fields will move to the right to make room for the Start date field.

Field:	Course code	Course name	Start date	Site	Sessions	Start date
Table:	Courses (S Ward)	Courses (S Ward)	Courses (S Ward)	Courses (S Ward)	Courses (S Ward)	Courses (S Ward)
Sort:			Ascending	Ascending		
Show:	☑	☑	☐	☑	☑	☑
Criteria:						
or:						

Figure 4.9 Two fields sorted in one order but displayed in the other order

4   Set the leftmost Start date field and the Site field to sort ascending.

5   Hide the leftmost Start date field by removing the tick from its Show box.

6   Save the query as **qrySortDateSite**.

7   Switch to datasheet view and check that the records are sorted first by start date, then by site within start date.

8   Close the query. Close the database.

Hint:

There is a convention that query names should start with the letters qry. This convention is particularly useful to more advanced designers of databases who write code and need to refer to their queries. It shows clearly what is a query and what is not. To be consistent and keep to the convention, we should really have given all our tables names starting with tbl. This book does not use the convention for tables, because table names in City & Guilds assignments do not usually use the convention.

→ Practise your skills 4.1: Books database

You will create queries to carry out searching and sorting on the Books table of your Books database. Look back at the methods earlier in this section if you need to. You will be asked to print the results of one query. There is no need to print them all.

1   Open your Books database.

2   All the queries described below should be based on your Books table. Print out a copy of your Books table if you do not already have an up-to-date copy. You will need this complete printout to help you check your queries.

3   Create a query to show books by Jane Austen, sorted in alphabetical order of Title. Show only the Author, Title and Price fields. Save the query as **qryAusten** and check the results.

4   Create a query to show books costing between £5 and £10 inclusive. Sort in ascending order of Price and show all the fields. (**Hint:** Do not use £ sign in queries on Number or Currency fields.) Save the query as **qryPriceBetween** and check the results.

5   Create a query to show books by Colin Dexter or John Le Carre. Sort in order of Year Published. Show the Stock No, Author and Title fields only. Save the query as **qryDexterLeCarre** and check the results.

6   Create a query to show books that are in stock and cost less than £10. Sort alphabetically by Author and show all the fields. Save the query as **qryInstockLessthan10** and check the results.

7   Create a query to show books that are out of stock or were published before 1990. Sort ascending by Author and by Year Published within Author. Show all the fields. Save the query as **qryOutofstockBef1990** and check the results. Print the results of this query using one sheet of paper.

8   Create a query to show books that cost £5.30 or more, but less than £9.99. Sort descending by Price. Show the Stock No, Author, Title and Year Published fields. Save the query as **qryMidPrice** and check the results.

9   Create a query to show books by authors with the initials C D. Use wildcards and remember that you can include spaces. Sort by Author and by Title within Author. Include all the fields. Save the query as **qryCD**.

10   Close the database and close down Access.

→ Practise your skills 4.2: Seeds database

You will create queries to carry out searching and sorting on the Seeds table of your Seeds database. Look back at the methods earlier in this section if you need to. You will be asked to print the results of one query. There is no need to print them all.

1 Open your Seeds database.

2 All queries will be based on your Seeds table. Print out a copy of your Seeds table if you do not already have an up-to-date copy. You will need this complete printout to help you check your queries.

3 Create a query to show seeds with a Price of £2.05 or more. Sort in ascending order of Name and show the CatNo, Name, Price and Height fields. Save the query as **qryPrice** and check the results.

4 Create a query to show seeds of flowers with a Height between 20 and 50 cm inclusive. Sort in ascending order of Height and show all the records. Save the query as **qryHeight** and check the results. Print the results of the query using one sheet of paper.

5 Create a query to show seeds that are Available, sorted in ascending order of Flowering Date and then in order of Name within Flowering Date. (**Hint:** Put the Flowering Date field in twice, but show it once.) Save the query as **qryAvailable** and check the results.

6 Create a query to show seeds of flowers with a Height of 40 cm or more that start flowering in July. Sort in ascending order of Height and show all the fields. Save the query as **qryJuly40** and check the results.

7 Create a query to show seeds that are not available or that cost less than £1. Sort in ascending order of Price and show all the fields. Save the query as **qryCheapNA** and check the results.

8 Create a query to show seeds of flowers with a Height greater than 20 cm and less than 50 cm. Sort in ascending order of Name. Show only the CatNo and Name fields. Save the query as **qryHeightGt20Lt50** and check the results.

9 Create a query to show seeds of flowers with a name that starts with 'Aster' or 'Snapdragon'. Sort in ascending order of CatNo and show all the fields. Save the query as **qryAsterSnapdragon** and check the results.

10 Close the database and close down Access.

→ Check your knowledge

1 What is the sign for 'greater than or equal to'?

2 What is the sign for 'less than or equal to'?

3 How can you include a field in a query but stop it from being displayed?

4 In a Date field of a query, how would you select dates between 01/01/98 and 01/06/99 inclusive?

5 How would you select dates after 01/01/98 and before 01/06/99, but not including those dates?

6 In a Number field of a query, you enter **15** in the Criteria row and **20** in the row just below it. When you have saved the query, how will Access rearrange your criteria?

7 If you set criteria on two fields and enter them in the same row, which logical operator will Access use, AND or OR?

8 You use the criterion **word*** in a Text field. Which of the following will be selected?
   - Learning Word
   - Word for Beginners
   - Wordsworth and his Poetry
   - The Sword in the Stone

9 You use the criterion ***word*** in a Text field. Which of the following will be selected?
   - Learning Word
   - Word for Beginners
   - Wordsworth and his Poetry
   - The Sword in the Stone

10 By convention, how should a query name start?

Section 5 | Action queries

You will learn to

- Extract selected records from a table into a new table in the same database
- Extract selected records from a table into an existing table in the same database
- Describe why data may need to be extracted from one database and stored in another database
- Select records for deletion and delete selected records from a database
- Find and replace the contents of fields using an update query
- Use an update query to carry out a calculation
- Find the default path for Access to save and find files
- Extract selected records to a new table in a different database file
- Append selected records to an existing table in a different database file

Information: Action queries

You have been using select queries to select and sort records. Select queries are the most basic kind of query. **Action queries** are used to change the contents of tables. There are four kinds of action query:

- A **make-table query** is used to copy selected records from one table into a new table.
- An **append query** is used to append (add) selected records from one table to another existing table.
- A **delete query** is used to delete selected records from a table.
- An **update query** is used to change the contents of selected records in a table. It can do the kind of simple text substitutions that you could do using Find and Replace. It can also do more complex substitutions involving calculations.

You start by creating a select query to select the records you want to delete, update, append or copy to a new table. You check the results of the select query to make sure that you have selected the right records. You then change your select query to the appropriate type of action query and complete the design. You run the action query and the actions take place. Finally you check to make sure that the right actions have been carried out on the data in the table.

Task 5.1 | Extract selected records from a table into a new table in the same database

You will put the records of evening classes from the Courses table into a new table called EveningClasses. You will do this by using a make-table query.

Method

1 Open your Courses database.
2 You should already have a query called qryEvening to select all the evening classes. Open the query. If you do not have qryEvening then create it now.
3 Check the results of the query again in datasheet view to make sure that all the right courses are shown. It is very important to check queries before turning them into action queries.
4 Switch back to design view.
5 Click on the Query menu to show the drop down list. Select Make-Table Query from the list.

Figure 5.1 The Query menu

6 The Make Table dialogue box appears. Key in the name of the new table: **EveningClasses**. Click OK.

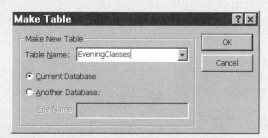

Figure 5.2 The Make Table dialogue box

7 You have prepared the action query, but it has not yet carried out its action. You must run it to make it work. To run the query, either click on the Query menu and select Run from the drop down list, or click the Run button on the toolbar. There should be a message saying that you are about to paste rows into a new table. Click Yes.
8 Close the query. When you are prompted to save it, answer No. You will still have the original qryEvening select query.
9 Click the Tables button in the database window to show the tables section. The new EveningClasses table should be listed.

Hint:

Do not look at datasheet view of an action query. It is unlikely to give you any useful information. Action queries are for running, not for viewing.

10   Open the EveningClasses table. It should have the same structure as the Courses table and contain all the evening class records that were selected by your query. You may need to make some minor alterations to the design to improve the display.

11   Adjust field widths if this is necessary to display all the data.

12   Logic (Yes/No) fields are likely to display 0 for false and −1 for true. The Evening field is probably displaying −1 in all records. Switch to design view and select the Evening field. In the Field Properties, change the format to True/False. Save the table design and switch to datasheet view to see that the Evening field now displays True.

13   Close the table.

Information: Check boxes

It is fine for the Evening field to display True or False, but you might like to know how to make it display check boxes. Start in design view, with the Evening field selected. In the Field Properties section of the window, click on the Lookup tab. Click the arrow to show the Display Control list and select Check Box.

General	Lookup	
Display Control	Text Box	▼
	Check Box	
	Text Box	
	Combo Box	

Figure 5.3 Display controls

Task 5.2	**Extract selected records from a table into an existing table in the same database**

There are some daytime part-time courses that are run in a similar way to evening classes. You will add these courses to the EveningClasses table using an append query.

Method

1   Create a query, based on the Courses table, to select courses that have between 10 and 12 sessions and are not evening classes. Remember to put both the criteria in the same row of the query design grid. Save the query as **qryDayLikeEvening**.

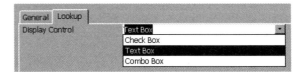

Site	Sessions	Start date	Price	Evening
Courses (S Ward)	Courses (S Ward)	Courses (S Ward)	Courses (S Ward)	Courses (S Ward)
☑	☑	☑	☑	☑
	Between 10 And 12			False

Figure 5.4 Criteria for 10 to 12 sessions, not evening

2   Check in datasheet view that the two courses C211a and C212 are shown.

3   Switch back to design view, click the Query menu and select Append Query from the drop down list.

4 The Append dialogue box appears. Use the arrow to show the drop down list of table names, and select EveningClasses. Click OK. Notice that an extra row, Append To, appears in the query design grid. It lists the field names in the EveningClasses table. They are exactly the same as the field names in the Courses table, so data entries can simply be copied from one field into another field with the same name.

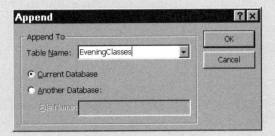

Figure 5.5 The Append dialogue box

5 Run the append query. You should see a message saying that you are about to append two rows. Click Yes.

6 Close the query without saving.

7 In the tables section of the database window, find and open the EveningClasses table. Check that it now contains the two extra records.

8 Close the table.

Information: Extracting data from one table to another

Database requirements change from time to time, and even the most carefully designed database may need to be modified. It may be necessary to split tables up. For example, suppose that a company keeps all its employee records in one table. A new Human Resources department is set up to deal with employees in the Northern region. Records of these employees need to be removed from the original table and put into a new separate table. After a time, the company decides to combine the Northern and Eastern regions. Records of Eastern region employees need to be removed from the main database and added to the Northern database.

If tables have the same structure then it is quite easy to extract data from one table to another. If the structures are different then it can be more difficult.

The copy and paste method of copying tables from Section 2 can be used if you want to:
- create an exact copy of a table with the same structure and all the same data
- create a copy of a table structure but not include any data
- append all the records from one table to an existing table with exactly the same structure.

You need to use a make-table query or an append query if you want to:
- copy selected records, but not all the records, from one table to a new table
- copy selected records, but not all the records, from one table to an existing table with the same structure →

- copy records from one table to another table with a slightly different structure
- copy selected records from one database file to another.

Append queries can be adjusted to cope with small differences in structure such as slightly different field names or a missing field. It may not be possible to copy records if there are big differences in the table structures.

Task 5.3 — Select records for deletion and delete selected records from a database

You will delete the Community Centre courses from the EveningClasses table, using a delete query.

Method

1 Open your Courses database. Create a new query using the EveningClasses table. Make sure that you add the EveningClasses table and not the Courses table when you first create the query.

2 Put in a criterion to select courses at the Community Centre site. Check in datasheet view that the right courses are selected. There should be three records.

3 Save the query as **qryEveCommunity**.

4 In design view, click on the Query menu and select Delete Query.

5 The design grid changes to look like Figure 5.6.

Field:	Course code	Course name	Site	Sessions
Table:	EveningClasses	EveningClasses	EveningClasses	EveningClasses
Delete:	Where	Where	Where	Where
Criteria:			"Community Centre"	
or:				

Figure 5.6 Design grid of a delete query

6 Run the query. You should see a warning message that you are about to delete three rows. This is right, so click Yes.

7 Close the query without saving changes.

8 Open the EveningClasses table and check that the Community Centre courses have gone.

9 Close the table.

Task 5.4 — Find and replace the contents of fields using an update query

You will change the name of the Community Centre to 'Hilltop Centre' in the Courses table.

Method

1. Create a query based on the Courses table.
2. Put in a criterion to select courses held at the Community Centre and save the query as **qryCourseCommunity**. (Although this query uses the same criterion as the qryEveCommunity query, it is based on a different table, so it is a separate query.)
3. Check in datasheet view that the right records are shown. There should be three records.
4. In design view, click the Query menu and select Update Query from the drop down list.
5. The design grid changes to show an Update To: row. Click in the Site column of this row, and key in **Hilltop Centre**.

Field:	Course code	Course name	Site	Sessions
Table:	Courses	Courses	Courses	Courses
Update To:			"Hilltop Centre"	
Criteria:			"Community Centre"	
or:				

Figure 5.7 Design grid of an update query

6. Run the query. You should see a warning message saying that you are about to update three rows. Click Yes.
7. Close the query without saving it.
8. Open the Courses table and check that the Community Centre has changed to Hilltop Centre.
9. Close the table.

Hint:

This is a simple replacement of text, and you could have used the Find and Replace facility in the Courses table as you did in Section 2. Some replacements need calculations. These must be carried out using an update query. Find and Replace will not do calculations.

Task 5.5 — Using an update query with a calculation

You will add £2 to the price of courses starting on or after 23rd September.

Method

1. Print out the Courses table on one sheet of paper. Write 'Before price increase' in pen on the printout.
2. Create a query based on the Courses table.
3. Put in a criterion to select courses starting on or after 23rd September.
4. Check in datasheet view that the right records are shown. There should be 10 records.
5. In design view, click on the Query menu and select Update Query from the drop down list.

6   Click into the Update To: row of the Price column and key in **[Price]+2**. For every selected record, the update query will take the value it finds in the Price field and add 2 to it. The square brackets are used to show that Price is a field name.

Field:	Site	Sessions	Start date	Price
Table:	Courses (S Ward)	Courses (S Ward)	Courses (S Ward)	Courses (S Ward)
Update To:				[Price]+2
Criteria:			>=#23/09/02#	
or:				

Figure 5.8 An update query using a calculation

7   Run the query. You should see a warning message saying that you are about to update 10 rows. Click Yes.

8   Close the query without saving it.

9   Open the Courses table.

10   Print out the Courses table on one sheet of paper. Write 'After price increase' in pen on the printout.

11   Check that £2 has been added to the price of courses starting on or after 23rd September.

12   Close the database and close down Access.

Hint:

Remember that you have to run an action query. People often create an action query and then wonder why it has not worked. They forgot to run it.

Information: Extracting records to a table in a different database

Make-table queries and append queries can be used to extract data to tables in a different database file. The method is similar to the method you used in Tasks 5.1 and 5.2 to extract data to tables in the same database file, but there is an added complication. Access needs to find the other database file. Unfortunately you have to key in the file name of the other database rather then selecting it from a list. You may also have to key in the path – the drive and folders containing the file.

Information: File names and paths

Every file has a name. It also has a path. The path is like an address, telling you where the file can be found. When you write a path, you start with the drive letter of the disk where the file is stored. A colon : always follows the drive letter. You then give the folder name. If there are several layers of folders, then you list them all, outermost folder first. The file name is written last. The backslash \ is used to separate the drive letter, the folder names and the file name:

C:\MyDocuments\Databases\CandG\Books.mdb

Drive C is the hard disk. It has a folder called MyDocuments. In this folder is another folder called Databases. Inside the Databases folder is another called CandG. Inside the CandG folder is a database file called Books.mdb.

Task 5.6	**Find out the default path for Access to save and find files**

When you first choose to save a new database, and when you start to open an existing database from within Access, there is a default folder which Access will use unless you choose a different folder. You can find out which this folder is. You can also change the default folder.

Method

1 Start Access. Open your Courses database.
2 Click on the Tools menu and select Options from the drop down list.
3 The Options dialogue box appears. It has a large number of tabs along the top. Click the General tab to bring it to the front.

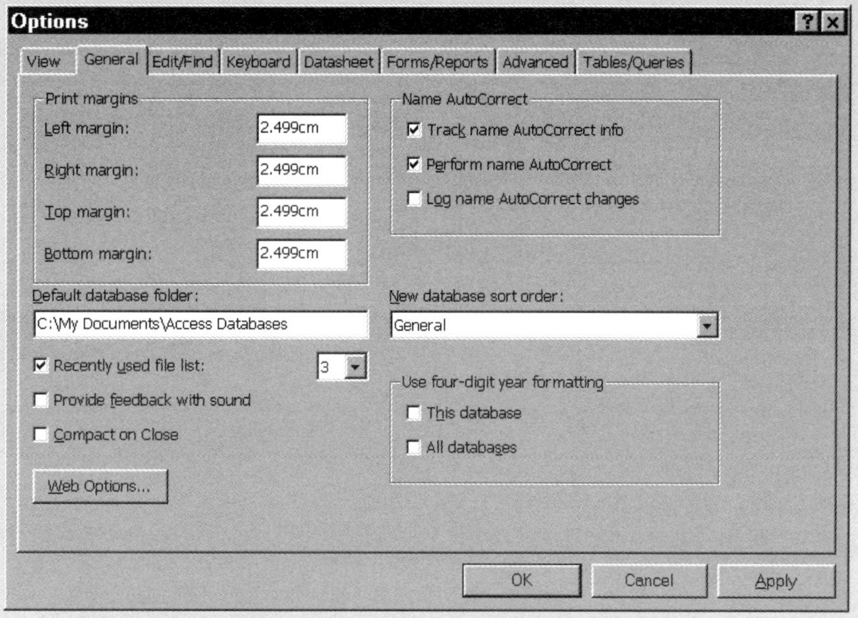

Options

View | General | Edit/Find | Keyboard | Datasheet | Forms/Reports | Advanced | Tables/Queries

Print margins
Left margin: 2.499cm
Right margin: 2.499cm
Top margin: 2.499cm
Bottom margin: 2.499cm

Name AutoCorrect
☑ Track name AutoCorrect info
☑ Perform name AutoCorrect
☐ Log name AutoCorrect changes

Default database folder:
C:\My Documents\Access Databases

New database sort order:
General

☑ Recently used file list: 3
☐ Provide feedback with sound
☐ Compact on Close

Use four-digit year formatting
☐ This database
☐ All databases

Web Options...

OK | Cancel | Apply

Figure 5.9 The Options dialogue box with the General tab in front

4 About halfway down on the left-hand side is a text box labelled 'Default database folder'. This shows the path to the default folder. In Figure 5.9 the default folder is C:\My Documents\Access Databases. Drive C: (the local hard disk) has a folder called My Documents. Inside this is a folder called Access Databases. This is where Access will look for database files unless it is given other instructions.
5 Make a note of the default folder on the computer you are using.
6 Click the Cancel button to close the dialogue box.

Task 5.7 — Extract selected records to a new table in a different database file

Hint:

If the More Courses.mdb database is not in the default folder, then you will need to key in the full path to the file, starting with the drive letter and putting in all the folders, separated by the backslash character. Examples: A:\More Courses.mdb; C:\My Documents\More Courses.mdb; N:\My Work\Databases\More Courses.mdb.

Hint:

Did Access have a problem finding the More Courses database? Check that you spelt its name correctly and included spaces if they are part of the name. If the database is not in the default folder, did you then enter the path correctly? If you get an error message and the query will not run, then close the query without saving. Open the original select query and convert it to a make-table query again. Enter the path and file name again.

In Task 5.1 you extracted records of evening classes from the Courses table and put them in a new table in the Courses database. Next you will extract the records of evening classes and put them in a new table in the More Courses.mdb database that you created in Section 2. The method is very similar to the method of Task 5.1, except that you have to let Access know which database the new table should be in. This is easiest if your More Courses.mdb database is in the default folder that you found in Task 5.6.

Method

1. Check that you have a More Courses.mdb database. If possible, put it in the default folder.
2. Open your Courses database. Open the qryEvening query. This should be your original select query that you used in Task 5.1.
3. Check the results of the query again in datasheet view.
4. Switch back to design view.
5. Click on the Query menu to show the drop down list. Select Make-Table Query from the list.
6. The Make Table dialogue box appears. Key in the name of the new table: **EveningClasses**. Choose the option for Another Database. Key in the file name of the database: **More Courses.mdb**. Click OK.
7. You have prepared the action query, but it has not yet carried out its action. To run the query, either click on the Query menu and select Run from the drop down list, or click the Run button on the toolbar. There should be a message saying that you are about to paste rows into a new table. Click Yes.
8. Close the query. When you are prompted to save it, answer No. You will still have the original qryEvening select query.
9. Close the Courses database and open the More Courses database. You should find that it contains a table called EveningClasses.
10. Open the EveningClasses table. It should have the same structure as the Courses table and contain all the evening class records that were selected by your query. You may wish to adjust field widths and to change the display in the logic field as you did in Task 5.1.
11. Close the table and close the More Courses database.

Task 5.8 — Append selected records to an existing table in a different database file

In Task 5.2, you used an append query to extract records from the Courses table and put them in another table in the same database. Next you will extract the records and append them to the existing EveningClasses table in the More Courses database.

Hint:

If the More Courses database is not in the default folder then you will need to key in the full path.

Hint:

You could consider copying records and pasting them into the other table as an alternative to using an append query.

Hint:

Perhaps the append query did not work. Maybe there was an error message saying 'Query must have at least one destination field'. This happens if you did not enter the table name and the file name and path correctly. Close the query without saving again. Check the exact spelling of the table name and the file name and try again. You should still have the qryDayLikeEvening query saved as a normal select query. Convert it to an append query again, and see if it works this time.

Method

1 Open the Courses database. Open the qryDayLikeEvening query that you created for Task 5.2.
2 Check in datasheet view that the correct two records are shown.
3 Switch back to design view, click the Query menu and select Append Query from the drop down list.
4 The Append dialogue box appears. Select the option button labelled Another Database. The File Name box appears. In this box, key in the name of the file More Courses.mdb.
5 There is an arrow to the right of the Table Name box. Click this arrow to show a drop down list. If Access has found the More Courses database file, then the tables in this database should be shown in the list. Select the EveningClasses table. Click OK.
6 A new row should appear in the query design grid, showing the field names in the EveningClasses table. They should be the same as the field names in the top row of the query design grid.
7 Run the append query. You should see a message 'You are about to append 2 rows'. Click Yes.
8 Close the query without saving again. Close the Courses database.
9 Open the More Courses database. Open the EveningClasses table and you should see the records that have been put in the table by the append query.
10 Close the More Courses database. Close down Access.

→ Practise your skills 5.1: Books database

You will use action queries to make some changes to your Books database. Save your select queries with suitable names before you convert them to action queries. You will also be copying records to a table in the Cardiff Books database that you created in Section 2.

1 Create a query based on your Books database that will select books in editions published before 1990.

2 Convert the query to a make-table query and use it to copy the selected records to a new table called **OldEditions**. (Add your name after the table name so that your name will appear on printouts.)

3 Create a query based on your Non Fiction table that will select books in editions published before 1990.

4 Convert the query to an append query and use it to copy the selected records to the OldEditions table.

5 Check that your OldEditions table contains the right records. Widen fields as necessary so that the data entries are shown in full. Make the logical field display Yes and No instead of 0 and 1.

6 Print the OldEditions table on one sheet of paper. Write Printout 1 in pen on the printout.

7 Create a query based on your OldEditions table to select books that are not in stock.

8 Convert the query to a delete query and use it to delete the books that are not in stock.　　　　　　　　→

9 Print the OldEditions table again on one sheet of paper. Write Printout 2 in pen on the printout.

10 Create a query based on the Books table to select books by C Dickens.

11 Convert the query to an update query and use it to replace C Dickens with Charles Dickens in all the selected records.

12 Create a query based on the Books table to select books costing more than £10.

13 Convert the query to an update query and use it to take 50p off the price of books costing more than £10. (**Hint:** Use [Price]-0.50.)

14 Print your Books table, sorted in ascending order of Price, on one sheet of paper. Write Printout 3 on the printout.

15 Use an append query to copy all the records for books by Jane Austen to the Books table of the Cardiff Books database. Check that the records have been copied successfully.

16 Close Access.

→ Practise your skills 5.2: Seeds database

You will use action queries to make some changes to your Seeds database. You will need to create and save suitable select queries before converting them to the appropriate kind of action queries.

1 Open your Seeds database.

2 Select the Dahlias from the Seeds table and copy their records to a new table called **SelectedFlowers**. (Use a make-table query.)

3 Select the Asters from the Seeds table and copy their records to the SelectedFlowers table. (Use an append query.)

4 Adjust the design of the SelectedFlowers table to improve the display.

5 Print the SelectedFlowers table, sorted in ascending order of Height, on one sheet of paper. Write Printout 1 on the printout.

6 Select seeds that are not available from the SelectedFlowers table and delete them. (Use a delete query.)

7 Print the SelectedFlowers table again, sorted in ascending order of Height, on one sheet of paper. Write Printout 2 on the printout.

8 Select all the available seeds from the Seeds table. Add 10p to the price of selected seeds. (**Hint:** Use [Price]+0.10.)

9 Print the Seeds table, sorted in order of CatNo, on one sheet of paper. Write Printout 3 on the printout.

10 Create a new database file called **Seeds2003** in the same folder as your Seeds database. Close the new database file.

11 Return to your Seeds database.

12 Export the structure (definition) only of your Seeds table to the Seeds2003 database. Call the new table **CurrentYearSeeds**.

13 Open the Seeds2003 database, and open the CurrentYearSeeds table. Enter the following data.

CatNo	Name	Price	Start Flowering	Available	Height (cm)
AX0401	Poppy Angels Choir	£2.85	01/07/03	Yes	60.00
AX0402	Poppy Danish Flag	£1.39	01/07/03	Yes	70.00
AX0403	Poppy Venus	£1.05	01/07/03	Yes	100.00

Table 5.1 Data for CurrentYearSeeds table

14 Return to your Seeds database. Use an append query to select records of Snapdragons and Asters and append them to the CurrentYearSeeds table in the Seeds2003 database.

15 Print your CurrentYearSeeds table.

16 Close the databases and close down Access.

→ Check your knowledge

1 What are the four types of action query that you have used?

2 You have just run a delete query. Can you use the Undo button to get the deleted records back?

3 What can you do with an update query that you cannot do with Find and Replace?

4 What is a potential problem with saving action queries?

5 How can you safely inspect a saved action query without running it?

6 You can append records from one table to another by using Copy and Paste, and choosing the Append option. What is the advantage of using an append query instead?

7 Why would you use a delete query rather than going through the table and deleting the unwanted records individually?

8 What is the advantage of using a make-table query rather than using Copy and Paste and choosing Structure and Data?

9 An employees table has a Salary field. You create an update query to add £500 to the salaries of selected employees. What would you key into the Update row of the Salary field?

10 What is a potential additional complication when you create an append query to append to a table in a different database?

You work for a holiday company that owns villas and holiday cottages for rent. You are asked to create a database to hold details of the villas and then make some changes.

1 Look at the data in Table 5.2. On paper, create a design for a table to hold the data. Show field names, data types, field sizes and formats. Set out your design as shown in Table 5.3. Choose a suitable field to be the primary key and make a note of this on your design.

VillaID	Villa Name	Country	Area	Sleeps	Renovated	Weekly Rental High	Weekly Rental Low	Renting this year
E20	Mon Repos	France	Normandy	6	12/11/01	£521.00	£411.00	Yes
E21	Bellevue	France	Normandy	4	12/11/01	£402.00	£356.00	Yes
E35	Villa Garcia	Spain	Costa del Sol	8	06/02/02	£600.00	£520.00	Yes
E36	Villa Juan	Spain	Costa del Sol	6	10/02/00	£550.00	£500.00	Yes
E37	Villa Rosita	Spain	Costa Brava	4	03/01/03	£420.00	£400.00	Yes
E38	Villa Bianca	Spain	Costa Brava	6	10/03/00	£560.00	£500.00	Yes
U44	Cosy Nook	England	Lake District	2	28/01/02	£380.00	£350.00	Yes
U45	Rose Cottage	England	Lake District	6	12/12/00	£600.00	£560.00	Yes
U46	Heron's View	England	Lake District	8	06/02/02	£640.00	£600.00	Yes
U47	Lakeside	England	Lake District	4	04/01/00	£510.00	£480.00	Yes
U48	Sea View	England	Cornwall	4	05/02/01	£500.00	£480.00	Yes
U49	Redruth	England	Cornwall	6	07/03/00	£580.00	£500.00	Yes

Table 5.2 Data for the Villas table

Field Name	Data Type	Field Size/Format

Table 5.3 Layout for design of the Villas table

Remember:

You add your name to the table name in order to identify your printouts.

2 Start Access and create a new database called **Villas**. Create a new table according to your design and save it as **Villas (Your name)**. Set a suitable primary key as shown in your design.

3 Enter the data from Table 5.2 into your Villas table.

4 Print the table in landscape orientation on one sheet of paper. Write Printout 1 on the printout.

5 Use the documenter to print out the table structure. This is Printout 2.

6 Use Find and Replace to find all the villas or cottages with an ID starting with U, and add an extra character so that the ID starts with UK. The number part of the ID should not change. (**Hint:** You need to match part of the field.)

7 Create an index with Country as the primary sort field and Area as the secondary sort field. Sort the table by Country and by Area within Country.

8 Print the sorted table on one sheet of paper (Printout 3).

9 Add three more cottages as shown below. Print the table again, sorted by Country and Area as before (Printout 4). Close the table.

VillaID	Villa Name	Country	Area	Sleeps	Renovated	Weekly Rental High	Weekly Rental Low	Renting this year
UK50	The Bluebells	England	Cornwall	6	06/01/03	£600.00	£560.00	Yes
UK51	Two Bridges	England	Lake District	4	12/02/03	£500.00	£470.00	Yes
E22	Saint Michel	France	Normandy	8	18/02/03	£650.00	£600.00	Yes

Table 5.4 Additional data for the Villas table

10 Create a new database file called **Cottages**. Save it in the same folder as your Villas database. Close this new database.

11 Return to your Villas database. Export the structure (definition) of the Villas table to the Cottages database. Give the new table the name **UKCottages**.

12 Open your Cottages database and open your UKCottages table. Check that it has the same structure as the Villas table but contains no records.

13 Enter the following records into your UKCottages table.

VillaID	Villa Name	Country	Area	Sleeps	Renovated	Weekly Rental High	Weekly Rental Low	Renting this year
UK701	Bwthyn Bach	Wales	Pembs	4	03/02/01	£500.00	£450.00	Yes
UK702	Henllan House	Wales	Pembs	8	03/11/02	£680.00	£600.00	Yes
UK703	Afal Mawr	Wales	Pembs	4	04/12/00	£500.00	£450.00	Yes
UK704	Cwm Tydu	Wales	Pembs	4	17/01/01	£500.00	£450.00	Yes

Table 5.5 Data for the UKCottages table

14 Close the Cottages database and return to the Villas database.

15 Create a query to select properties in England. Append these properties to the UKCottages table in the Cottages database. You could use an append query or you could copy and paste the records.

16 Print the UKCottages table, sorted in order of renovation date, on one sheet of paper (Printout 5).

17 Use a delete query to delete the properties in England from the Villas table in the Villas database.

18 Delete the Renovated field from the UKCottages table in the Cottages database.

19 Add a field to the UKCottages table. The field name is **Start Rentals**. The data type is Date/Time, and the format is Short Date.

20 In the UKCottages table, change the field name VillaID to **CottageID**. Change the field name Villa Name to **Cottage Name**.

21 Enter the following data into the UKCottages table.

CottageID	Cottage Name	Start Rentals
UK44	Cosy Nook	23/03/03
UK45	Rose Cottage	23/03/03
UK46	Heron's View	30/03/03
UK47	Lakeside	23/03/03
UK48	Sea View	30/03/03
UK49	Redruth	30/03/03
UK50	The Bluebells	23/03/03
UK51	Two Bridges	23/03/03
UK701	Bwthyn Bach	23/03/03
UK702	Henllan House	30/03/03
UK703	Afal Mawr	30/03/03
UK704	Cwm Tydu	23/03/03

Table 5.6 Additional data for the UKCottages table

22 Print the UKCottages table, sorted by CottageID, on one sheet of paper (Printout 6).

23 Create a query to select cottages in Cornwall or Pembrokeshire that sleep 4 people. Sort by cottage name. Print out only the CottageID, Cottage Name, Area, Weekly Rental High and Weekly Rental Low fields (Printout 7).

24 Use an update query to add £10 to the Weekly Rental High field of cottages that start rentals on 30/03/03.

25 Print the UKCottages table, sorted by CottageID, on one sheet of paper (Printout 8).

26 Close down Access.

Section 6 | Forms

You will learn to

- Create a data entry form
- Save a form
- Use a form for inputting of data
- Use a form for editing of data
- Modify the design of a form
- Add a header and footer to a form
- Format text on a form
- Add and delete fields on a form
- Change the background colour of a form
- Add a picture to a form
- Print a form
- Describe the importance of user-friendly design when creating a form

Information: Database forms

People who work on data entry to a database do not usually enter the data directly into the table. It is normal for the database developer to provide a data entry form on the screen, often showing one record at a time. The form is linked to a table so that the entries on the form are stored in the table. Forms are also used to view and edit data.

Access provides a wizard to help you create data entry forms. Use the wizard. It is much easier than creating a form on your own. You can then alter the form design to meet the requirements of the database users.

Task 6.1 | Create a data entry form

You will create a data entry form for the Courses table. We will go through the wizard slowly the first time, looking at the different options.

Method

1	Open your Courses database.
2	Click on the Forms button in the database window so that the Forms section shows.
3	Double click on 'Create form by using wizard'. The first dialogue box of the wizard appears.

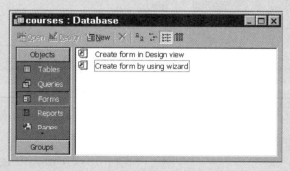

Figure 6.1 Forms section of the database window

4 Click the arrow in the Tables/Queries box to see the drop down list of tables and queries. It is important to choose the right table or query for your form. Select the Courses table from the list.

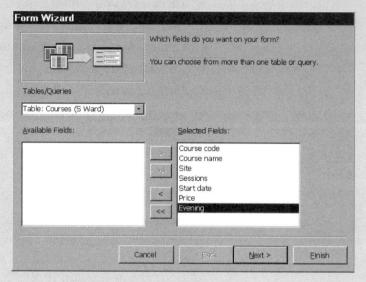

Figure 6.2 Form Wizard dialogue 1

5 Add all the fields to the form design. You can add fields one at a time by selecting them and clicking the single right pointing arrow. To add all the fields at once, click the double right pointing arrow. You can remove a field from the design by selecting it and clicking the left pointing arrow.

6 Click Next. The second dialogue box of the wizard appears.

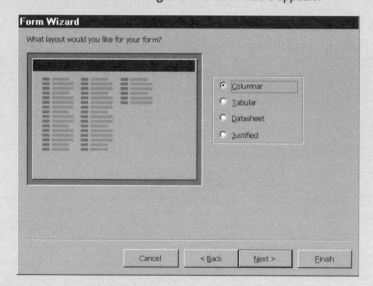

Figure 6.3 Form Wizard dialogue 2

7 By default, a columnar layout is selected for the form. This is the most common choice and lets you display one record at a time. Click on the other three options to see an idea of the layout in the display area. Select Columnar again.

8 Click Next. The third dialogue box of the wizard appears.

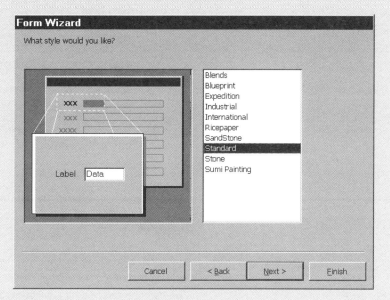

Figure 6.4 Form Wizard dialogue 3

9 You can now choose a ready-made style for your form. Click on each of the options to see what is available. This time, click back on Standard.

10 Click Next. The fourth dialogue box of the wizard appears.

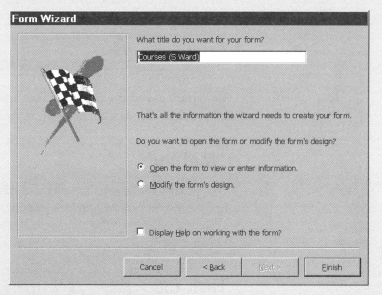

Figure 6.5 Form Wizard dialogue 4

11 The final step asks you to give a title to the form. By default it offers the name of the table or query that you used to create the form. Whatever you key into the title box will be used as a name for the form and also as a title to be displayed in the title bar. By convention, form names begin with the letters frm. Key the name **frmCourses** into the box. There is no need to include your own name in a form name. You will be able to put your name in a footer later.

12 The option 'Open the form to view or enter information' should be selected.

13 Click Finish. Wait while the wizard creates the form.

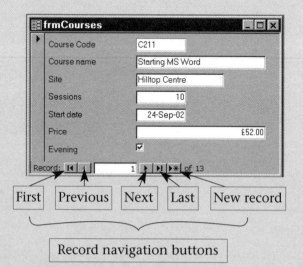

Figure 6.6 The form created by the wizard

14 The form appears in **form view**. This is the usual view of the form. It lets you see the data from the table. The form displays the first record from the table. You can use the record navigation buttons to see the other records. The buttons look a bit like video or tape recorder controls. You can move forward to the next record, back to the previous record, straight to the first or last record, or you can go to a new empty record. Use the buttons to navigate between the records so that you see how they work.

Task 6.2 Save a form

The wizard saved the form for you, using the name that you gave it. You will need to save the form again if you make any changes to its design.

Method

1 Click the Save button on the toolbar to save the latest version of the form and replace the previous version.

Task 6.3 Use a form for inputting of data

You will enter two new records using the form.

Method

1 Click on the 'New record' navigation button. This is the button on the right, with the star and the arrow. The form should clear, ready for you to enter a new record. The only entries left in the white boxes should be default values.

2	The flashing cursor should already be in the Course code box. If not, then click into the box. Key in **C412** then press the Tab key. (The Tab key is on the left of the keyboard and shows two arrows.) The cursor should move to the next white box.
3	Key in **MS Excel at Work**. Tab down to the next box, which should already contain the default value **Riverside**. Tab again.
4	Continue entering data:

Sessions: 20
Start date: 12/09/02
Price: £75
Evening: Yes. Click to place a tick in the check box.

5	As you tab away from the Evening box, the record is saved and a new empty record appears. Enter data into the new record:

Course code: C213a
Course name: Starting Publisher
Site: Hilltop Centre
Sessions: 11
Start date: 24/09/02
Price: £62
Evening: Yes.

6	Tab to move to a new record, or click a navigation button to move to an existing record. The record you have just entered is saved when you move out of it.

Task 6.4 — Use a form for editing of data

You will use the form to change the starting date of C419, Creating a web page.

Method

1	Click into the Course code box. It does not matter which record is on the screen.
2	Click on the Edit menu and select Find from the drop down menu.
3	The Find and Replace dialogue box appears. Key in **C419** into the Find What box. Click the Find Next button, then click the Cancel button to close the dialogue box.
4	The record for course C419 should show on the form.
5	Click into the Start date box and change the date to 26-Sep-02.
6	Save the change by using a navigation button to move to a different record.

Hint:

Instead of selecting Find from the Edit menu, you can click the Find button on the toolbar. It is the button with the picture of binoculars.

The form is fine to use as it is, but you can change its appearance. You will modify the form design by moving the boxes where you enter data.

Method

I   Change to design view of the form, using the View button on the toolbar. You may need to make the design view window a bit larger to see the whole of the form. To make a window larger, point the mouse at the window border until the mouse pointer looks like a double-headed arrow, then drag the mouse until the window is big enough.

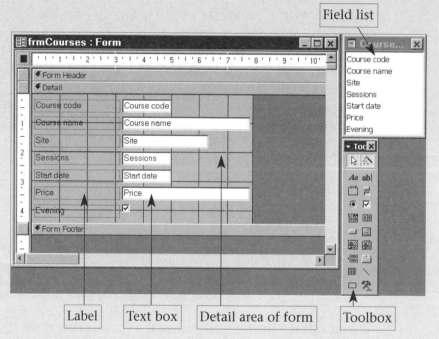

Figure 6.7 The form in design view

2   Look at the form in design view. Find the Detail section. This contains labels showing the field names. It contains text boxes which also show the field names in design view. In form view these text boxes show the data from the table. These text boxes are linked to the fields of the table. Labels are not linked to the table. They contain normal text.

3   There should be a toolbox and a field list displayed in their own little windows. If the toolbox is not showing, click on the View menu and select Toolbox from the drop down list. If the field list is not showing, select it from the View menu in the same way. You can move a window on the screen by pointing the mouse to its title bar and holding down the left button as you drag the window to its new position. You may need to move the toolbox or the field list if they are hiding part of the form.

4   You can change the size of a label. Click into the Course code label to select it. Black squares, the **resize handles,** appear at the corners and on the sides of the label. In the top left corner of the label and the text box is a larger black square which is used for moving the label or text box. Point the mouse to one of the smaller black squares. The mouse pointer changes to a double-headed arrow. Hold the left button down, and drag to change the size of the label. Then drag the label back to its starting size.

Figure 6.8 The Course code label with resize handles

5   You can move a label with its text box. Point the mouse to the edge of the label, but not to a black square. The mouse pointer should change to a black hand with the fingers spread out. Hold the left button down and drag to move the label with its text box. Then put the label back where it started.

6 You can move a label on its own, without its text box. Point the mouse to the large black square in the top left corner of the label. The mouse pointer should change to a hand with a pointing finger. Hold the left button down and drag to move the label on its own. Move the label back to where it started.

7 Click on the Course code text box to select it. Its resize handles appear. You can resize a text box, and you can move it with or without its label. Try it out.

8 Move text boxes with their labels so that there are two columns on the form as shown in Figure 6.9. As you move a text box over the edge of the form, the form will get wider to make room for it. You may need to widen the window yourself so that you can still see the whole of the form.

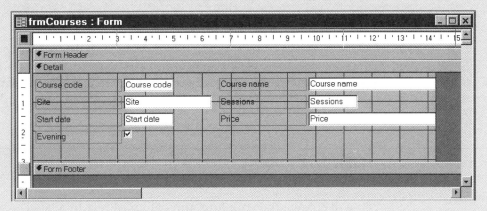

Figure 6.9 The form with rearranged text boxes and labels

Hint:

Moving and resizing labels and text boxes can take a lot of practice. It needs careful control of the mouse and many people find it awkward at first. You may find it easier to move text boxes if you do not select them first, but just aim the mouse at the box and drag straight away. If you select a label or text box and then accidentally click into it, you will place a cursor for keying in and you will not be able to move the label or text box. If this happens, click outside the label or text box to deselect it, then try again.

Task 6.6 — Add a header and footer to a form

You will add a title in a header and add your name in a footer.

Method

1 There should be a grey bar labelled Form Header, but there may not be any space for the header above the Detail section. Point the mouse to the lower edge of the grey bar labelled Form Header. The mouse pointer should change to a bar with a double-headed arrow. Hold down the left button and drag the mouse down a short distance to create space for a header.

Figure 6.10 Dragging down to create space for a header

2 Point the mouse to the lower edge of the grey bar labelled Form Footer. Drag down to create space for a footer.

3 Now look at the toolbox and find the Label button Aa. Click on the Label button. Point the mouse to the Form Header area. The mouse pointer should look like a cross with a letter A near it. Draw a rectangle by holding down the left mouse button as you drag the mouse down and to the right.

4 You now have a label with a flashing cursor in it. Key in **Computer Courses**.

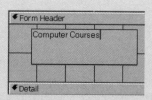

Figure 6.11 Header with a label

5   Click outside the label to deselect it.
6   Click on the Label button in the toolbox again. Draw a label in the Form
     Footer area and key in your name.
7   Switch to form view using the View button on the toolbar. Your header and
     footer should be displayed. Switch back to design view.
8   Save the design changes by clicking the Save button on the toolbar.

Task 6.7   Format text on a form

You will change the size, font and colour of text in a label.

Method

I   Click on the label in the header to select it. The black handles should appear.
2   Use the buttons on the Formatting toolbar to choose a different font, make the font larger and bold, centre the
     text in the label and change the font colour. You might put a background colour in the label and give the label a
     coloured border. Some of the buttons have arrows beside them. Click the arrow to see a drop down list of
     options or a palette of colours. Experiment until you are happy with your title.

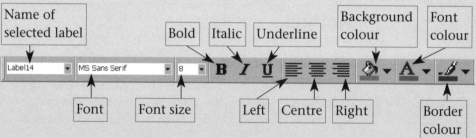

Figure 6.12 The Formatting toolbar

3   Switch to form view to see how your changed form looks.
4   The labels in the details section of the form and the label in the footer can also be formatted. So can the text
     boxes. You might like to try this if you have time. Do not use too many different formats or the form will be
     cluttered and difficult to read.

Hint:

Take care not to click into the label and place a cursor for keying in. If you do this
you will not be able to use the Formatting toolbar. Click outside the label to
deselect it, then select it again.

Task 6.8   Add and delete fields on a form

If you add or delete a field in the table on which the form is based, then you will need to add or delete the field on the form too. In this task, you will not alter the table design, but will just delete a field from the form and then add it in again.

Method

1	In design view, select the Course name label. Press the Delete key on the keyboard. The label disappears. Select the Course name text box. Press the Delete key on the keyboard. The text box disappears. Switch to form view to confirm that the Course name field is no longer shown. Switch back to design view.
2	The field list should be showing. This is a small window giving the names of all the fields, as shown in Figure 6.7. If the field list is not showing, then click on the View menu and select Field List.
3	Point the mouse to the field list and select Course name. Drag Course name to the form and drop it where the Course name text box used to be. Both a text box and a label appear. You can adjust their position if necessary.
4	Check in form view that the Course name is shown correctly on the form as it was originally.
5	In form view, click into the Course code field. Press the Tab key. Instead of moving to Course name, you move to Site. Carry on pressing the Tab key. You should find that the Course name field now comes last in the tab order. This is not convenient for the user.
6	To adjust the tab order, switch to design view and select Tab Order from the View menu. A list of field names appears with Course name at the bottom. Select Course name in the list by clicking in the grey area to the left of the Course name. With the mouse pointing to the grey area, drag Course name up the list until it is just below Course code. Click OK. Save the form design.
7	Check in form view that the tab order is now correct.

Task 6.9   Change the background colour of a form

You will give your form a coloured background.

Method

1	In design view, click into the details section of the form but not on a label or text box. Use the Background Colour button on the toolbar to choose a colour.
2	Click into the header section and choose the same colour, then do the same with the footer section.
3	Look at the effect in form view.

Task 6.10 — Add a picture to a form

You will add a picture to decorate your form.

Method

1 Before you start, you will need to have a picture (image) file saved in a folder where you can find it. Ask your tutor where you can find a suitable image file.

2 In design view, look at the toolbox and find the Image button ![] . Make sure you choose the right button. There are two others that look similar but have no mountains on them. Click on the Image button.

3 Point the mouse to a suitable empty area in the header or footer and draw a rectangle. The Insert Picture dialogue box appears.

4 Find and open the folder containing your image file. Select the image file and click OK.

5 The picture that appears in the image box may not be the right size. To make the picture fit the box, you need to alter one of its properties. Right click on the picture and select Properties from the pop-up list. A window appears showing a list of properties of the image box. Look for the Size Mode property. It is probably set to Clip. Click into the Size Mode box to show the arrow. Click the arrow to show the drop down list and select Zoom. Close the properties window by clicking the button in its top right corner.

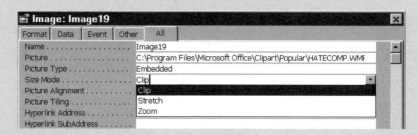

Figure 6.13 The properties window for an image box

6 Your image should now be resized to fit in its box, but it should keep its proportions.

7 Another way of finding a picture is to use the clipart gallery. Click into the area of the form where you want the picture. Click on the Insert menu and choose Object from the drop down list.

8 The Insert Object dialogue box appears. Scroll down the list to Microsoft Clip Gallery and select it. Click OK.

9 The clip gallery opens. Select a suitable picture from the clip gallery and insert it.

10 You will probably need to resize the picture and change its Size Mode property to Zoom as you did before.

11 Switch to form view to see the effect.

Task 6.11 | Print a form

You will print forms showing all the records, then you will print one form showing one record.

Method

1. In form view, find the record for course C413, Using Publisher.
2. Click the Print Preview button on the toolbar or select Print Preview from the File menu.
3. If you get a message saying that the section width is greater than the page width then your form is too wide to fit on the page. Go back to design view and try to make your form less wide by dragging the right-hand border of the form to the left. Print preview again. If you cannot make your form narrow enough to fit, then use landscape orientation (File, Page Setup, Page tab).
4. The records are probably displayed one after another, taking up two or three pages, depending on how big you have made the forms.
5. Click the Print button on the toolbar to print all the records. Click the Close button on the toolbar to return to form view.
6. To print one form, click on the File menu to show the drop down list, and select Print. The Print dialogue box appears. Do not use the Print button on the toolbar this time because it does not show the dialogue box.

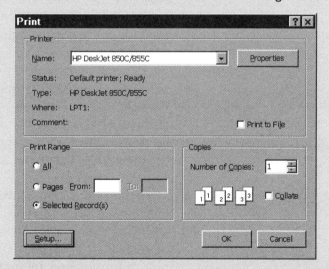

Figure 6.14 Print dialogue box

7. In the Print Range section of the dialogue box, select 'Selected Record(s)'. Click OK.
8. This time only one form should print, showing the record for course C413.
9. Close the form and close down Access.

Information: User friendly design

There are many formatting methods you can use to change the appearance of a form, and many objects you can put on a form to decorate it. These features are available, but that does not mean that you should use them. It is usually better to keep the form quite simple. Remember the purpose of the form. It is to help the user to enter, edit and view the records from the table. The form should be **user friendly**. That is, the form should be easy and pleasant to use.

Here are some points to consider when designing a form.

- Who is going to use your form? People who use it every day as part of their job? Members of the general public who will use it once and never again? Serious people with work to do? Fun loving people in their spare time? You and nobody else ever?
- Where is the database user getting the data? If it comes from a paper form, then it could help if your form on the screen has a similar layout to the paper form.
- The text should be clear and easy to read. Use at most two different fonts, perhaps one for the title and one for the main detail area.
- Every data entry box should have a clear descriptive label showing what should be entered there. If the field names are not clear enough then you could enter a better description in the labels.
- Use a layout and spacing so that the user's eye follows naturally from top left to bottom right, as the data is read or entered. (At least do this for users from a culture where they read from left to right.)
- Try to avoid making the form look overcrowded.
- Most users like to tab from one data entry box to the next rather than clicking with the mouse. Make sure that the Tab key leads to the right box. Change the tab order if necessary.
- Be careful with your use of colour. A colour scheme that seems bright and cheerful to one person can seem horribly garish and tiring to another person.
- Most people don't much like typing, they find it difficult to remember exactly what to type, and they are likely to make keying-in errors. Where possible, you might let them click option buttons or check boxes, or select from a drop down list. You have not yet learned how to use these features on a form, but it is something you might learn in the future.

Data entry is not a thrilling job at the best of times. The database user may have to spend many hours using the form that you design. Make his or her life easier by designing a good, user-friendly form.

→ Practise your skills 6.1: Books database

You will create a form based on the Books table and use it to enter and edit records.

1 Open the Books database.
2 Use the wizard to create a form based on the Books table. Include all the fields. Use columnar layout. Use the standard style. Give the form the title **frmBooks**.

3 Add a new record:

Stock No:	41
Author:	Terry Pratchett
Title:	The Colour of Magic
Price:	£5.99
In Stock:	No
Year Published:	1998

4 Find the record of Life at Thrush Green by Miss Read. There is a new edition. Change the year published to 2002, the price to £10.50 and In Stock to yes.

5 Move the text boxes and labels on the form so that they appear in two columns as shown in Figure 6.15.

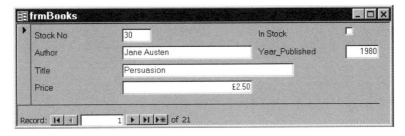

Figure 6.15 Layout of the frmBooks form

6 Add the title **Books for Sale** in a header. Use a suitable font and size for the title.

7 Add your name in a footer.

8 Add a picture to the form.

9 Make any further formatting changes to improve the appearance of the form, and save the new design.

10 Print out the form showing one record only: the record of Life at Thrush Green.

11 Delete the author field from the form. Add the Author field in again and adjust the tab order.

12 Close the form and close down Access.

→ **Practise your skills 6.2:** Seeds database

You will create a form based on the Seeds table and use it to enter and edit records.

1 Open your Seeds database.

2 Use the wizard to create a form based on the Seeds table. Include all the fields. Use columnar layout. Use the standard style. Give the form the title **frmSeeds**.

3 Alter the layout of the form so that the labels and text boxes appear in two columns as shown in Figure 6.16.

Figure 6.16 Layout of the frmSeeds form

4 Add a header with the title **Seeds by Mail Order**. Use a suitable font and size.

5 Add a footer with your name. Save the design changes.

6 Add a new record:

    CatNo: AX0361
    Name: Lupin Lulu Mixed
    Price: £1.85
    Start Flowering: 1/6/03
    Available: Yes
    Height (cm):   60

7 Find the record AX0334, Aster Pink Fizz. Seeds are now available at a new price of £1.55. Make the changes.

8 Print out the form showing all the records. It will probably take two pages, depending on how big you have made the form.

9 Print out one record only: the record for Aster Pink Fizz.

10 Close the form and close down Access.

→ **Check your knowledge**

1 What are forms normally used for?

2 If you enter data into a form, where will the data be stored?

3 Can you base a form on a query?

4 What is the conventional start of a form name?

5 Why is the design of a form important?

Section 7 | Reports

You will learn to

- Identify the use of a report for presenting information
- Create a tabular report showing all fields
- Add a header and footer to a report
- Save and print a report
- Create a columnar report showing selected fields
- Create a report showing selected records
- Create a report showing selected fields and records
- Format fields in a report
- Add, delete and rearrange fields
- Add a total to a report
- Change the sorting order of a report
- Create a report with grouped data and subheadings
- Add an image to a report

Information: Database reports

A database report displays data for printing. When you print a table, you have very little control over the layout and appearance of the printout. If you create a report to display the data from the table, you can control exactly what is printed and where it is printed.

It is possible to create a report based directly on a table. The disadvantage is that you cannot choose which records to print. You have to print them all. A better method is to create a query to select the records you want, then create a report based on the query. If you want to use the same report to print a different selection of records then you change the query but keep the report the same. It is important to remember which query belongs to which report. You could name the query to show which report depends on it.

Access provides a wizard to help you design reports. Use the wizard to produce reports. You can then change the design if it is not quite what you want. This is much easier than creating a report design by yourself. An even easier and quicker method is to use an autoreport. This uses default settings to create a basic report.

<table>
<tr><td>Task 7.1</td><td>Create a tabular report showing all fields</td></tr>
</table>

You will create a query and use it to create a report showing all the fields and all the records from your Courses table. You will use an autoreport to create the report.

Method

1 Open your Courses database.
2 Create a new query based on the Courses table. Include all the fields. Do not put in any criteria because we want to show all the records at first. Save the query with the name **qryForRptCourses**. The name is chosen to show that the query is used for a report called rptCourses. Check the query in datasheet view to make sure that it does show all the records correctly. Close the query.
3 Click the Reports button in the database window to show the reports section of the database.

Figure 7.1 The reports section of the database window

4 Click the New button in the database window. The New Report dialogue box appears.
5 Select Autoreport: Tabular from the list of options.
6 Click the arrow in the box labelled 'Choose the table or query where the object's data comes from'. Select your qryForRptCourses query from the drop down list.
7 Click OK and wait for the report to be created. It appears in preview view.
8 The report should have a title, which will be the same as the name of the query. You can change this title later. It should show all the field names. Below the field names, all the records should be displayed. Today's date and the page number appear in a footer. Click on the report to zoom in or out so that you can see the complete page layout as well as the detail. Apart from the title, this report is quite acceptable for printing.
9 Switch to design view of the report by clicking the View button on the toolbar.

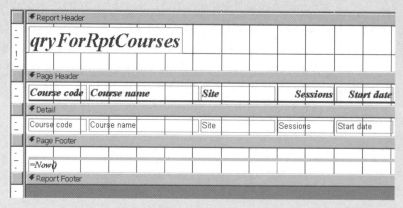

Figure 7.2 Part of the report design window

10   Look at the report design. It is similar to the form design in many ways. There is a main design window. There should also be a toolbox in its own window. There may be a field list and a list of properties headed Report. You can move these windows if they are covering up part of the main window. If any of the windows are missing, click on the View menu and select them from the drop down list.

11   Look at the report design. There are several sections:

- The report header is printed once only, on the first page of the report. It contains a label with the title of the report.
- The page header is printed at the top of every page of the report. The current report has only one page, but most reports will have several pages. The page header contains labels showing the field names.
- The details section is the main part of the report. It contains text boxes linked to the fields in the query. In design view these text boxes show the field names. In preview the text boxes show the data from the fields, and there is a row for each record.
- The page footer is printed at the bottom of every page of the report. It contains a text box on the left, showing a formula **=Now()**. This formula automatically finds the current date. In preview the current date is displayed. On the right of the page footer is another text box containing **="Page " & [Page] & " of " & [Pages]**. This produces the display **Page 1 of 1** in the preview.
- The report footer is printed once on the last page of the report. This report has nothing in the report footer.

Hint:

Sometimes part of a window can be off the screen. This can give problems if you want to use the scroll bar but it is not showing. Move the window by dragging its title bar until the scroll bar shows. If a scroll bar does not seem to work make sure that it belongs to the right window.

Task 7.2   Add a header and footer to a report

You will change the title in the report header and put your name in the page footer.

Method

1   Click on the title in the report header to select the label. Click again to place a cursor in the text. Delete the existing text and key in a new title: **Computer Courses**. Click out of the label to deselect it.

2   Click on the text box in the page footer showing **=Now()**. This text box does not have to be so big. Use the resize handles to make it smaller so that there is a space in the middle of the page footer.

3   Click the Label button in the toolbox and draw a label in the middle of the page footer. Key in your name in this label. Click out of the label to deselect it.

Hint:

You can move and resize labels and text boxes just as you did in the form design. You can make new labels using the toolbox. You can select a label and format its font, size and colour.

Task 7.3   Save and print a report

You will save and print your report on computer courses.

Method

1   Save the report design by clicking the Save button on the toolbar. This button appears in design view but not in preview. Give your report the name **rptCourses**.

Hint:

If you are asked to put the date or the page number in a header, copy the appropriate text box from the page footer to the page header. This is easier than remembering what to key into the text box.

In City & Guilds
instructions and elsewhere
you may see a report
called a 'report form'. This
means a report in Access
and not a form.

2 Switch to preview by clicking either on the View button or the Print Preview button on the toolbar. Check that the report is suitable for printing.

3 Click the Print button on the toolbar to print the report.

4 Close the report. You can use the X button in the top right corner of the report window (not the Access window), or you can select Close from the File menu.

Task 7.4	Create a columnar report showing selected fields

You will use the wizard to create a report showing the Course code, Course name, Site and Start date fields. This report will be based on its own new query.

Method

1 Create a query based on the Courses table. Include all the fields and do not put in any criteria. Save the query as **qryForRptStarting**. Close the query.

2 In the reports section of the database window, double click on 'Create report by using wizard'.

3 The first dialogue box of the wizard asks you to choose a table or query. Click the arrow to see the drop down list and select qryForRptStarting.

4 Select Course code from the Available fields list and use the arrow to move it to the Selected fields list. Move Course name, Site and Start date in the same way.

5 Click the Next button.

6 The second dialogue box of the wizard asks if you want grouping levels. It is possible to group records in a report. For example, you could group by site and have the Riverside courses in one group and the Hillside courses in another group. This report does not need any grouping so just click Next.

7 The third dialogue box asks if you want the records sorted. Show the drop down list in box 1 and select Start date. Click Next.

8 The fourth dialogue box asks you to choose a layout. The default is tabular, like the report you created earlier. Select the columnar layout. Keep the orientation as portrait. Click Next.

9 The fifth dialogue box asks you to choose a style. Select the different options to see what they look like, then select Corporate. Click Next.

10 The sixth and final dialogue box asks you to choose a title. This title will also be used as a name for saving the report. Key in **rptStarting**. You have a choice of previewing the report or changing the design. Choose to preview the report. Click Finish.

11 The wizard creates the report. It also saves the report using the name that you type in. This columnar report shows the records one after another down the page, and it probably has two or three pages. Check that the records have been sorted in order of starting date. Use the page navigation buttons at the bottom of the window to go to page 2.

12 Switch to design view and change the title to **Course Starting Dates**.

13 Add your name in the page footer.

14 Preview again, and print the report.

15 Save and close the report.

Task 7.5 — Create a report showing selected records

You will use your rptCourses report to show records of courses at the Riverside site. You do this by changing the query that you used to create the report. You do not need to change the report design at all.

Method

1	Open your qryForRptCourses query in design view.
2	Put in a criterion to select courses held at the Riverside site. Check in datasheet view that the correct records are selected.
3	Save the query, then close it.
4	In the reports section of the database window, select and open your rptCourses report in preview.
5	Check that only the Riverside courses are shown.
6	Print the report and close it.

Task 7.6 — Create a report showing selected fields and records

You will use the wizard to create a new tabular report showing the Course code, Course name, Site, Sessions and Evening fields. This report will be based on a new query that you can use to show selected records.

Method

1	Create a new query based on the Courses table. Include all the fields. Put in a criterion to select courses starting before 30/9/02. Check that the correct records are selected.
2	Save your query as **qryForRptSessions**. Close the query.
3	In the reports section of the database window, double click on 'Create report by using wizard'.
4	In the first dialogue box of the wizard, select qryForRptSessions as the query to be used. Select the fields Course code, Course name, Site, Sessions and Evening and move them to the Selected fields list. Click Next.
5	In the second dialogue box, just click Next.
6	In the third dialogue box, sort by Site in box 1 then Course name in box 2. Click Next.
7	In the fourth dialogue box, keep the tabular layout but change to landscape orientation. Click Next.
8	In the fifth box keep the corporate style. Click Next.
9	In the sixth box, key in the title **rptSessions**. Click Finish.
10	Look at the report. The fields have been arranged in the order Site, Course name, Course code, Sessions, Evening. If you ask the wizard to sort records, it will arrange the fields in the order you chose for sorting. The records are sorted first by Site and then by Course name, so these fields are displayed first.

| 11 | The report does not show the Start date field, but you should check that all the records are for courses starting before 30/9/02. Compare your report with the printout for rptCourses, or with a printout of the table. |

Task 7.7 — Format fields in a report

You will format labels and text boxes in your rptSessions report.

Method

1	Switch to design view of your rptSessions report.
2	Change the text in the title to '**Sessions booked for courses**'.
3	Select the label containing the title and use its resize handles to make the label wider. The right-hand edge of the label should be over the right-hand edge of the Evening field name label.
4	Keep the label selected. Use the Centre button on the Formatting toolbar to centre the title in its label.
5	The font in the label is probably Times New Roman, size 20, bold and italic. Use the Formatting toolbar to change this to Arial font, size 18, bold but not italic.
6	Select the labels containing the field names. You can select them all at once. Click on the first label, then hold down the Shift key as you click on each of the other labels. You can tell that the labels are selected because they show their resize handles.
7	Use the Formatting toolbar to change the selected labels to Arial font, size 10, bold but not italic.
8	Put your name in the page footer.
9	Select the labels and text boxes in the page footer and format them to Arial font, size 10, bold but not italic.
10	Switch to preview to see how your changes appear.
11	You may find that one or more of your field names do not show in full. Switch back to design view and make labels wider as necessary to show the names in full.
12	Save the changes to the design by clicking the Save button on the toolbar.

Hint:

Another method of selecting all the controls (such as labels or text boxes) in a row is to click in the left margin opposite the controls. You can select more than one row by dragging the mouse in the margin. You can also select controls in a column by clicking in the top margin.

Task 7.8 — Add, delete and rearrange fields

You will add the Price field to your rptSessions report, remove the Course code field, and rearrange some of the fields. You will also change to portrait orientation.

Method

| 1 | Start with your rptSessions report in design view. |
| 2 | The field list should be showing. If not, click on the View menu and select Field list from the drop down list. |

Figure 7.3 The field list

3   Select the Price field in the field list. Hold down the left mouse button as you drag the field into the report design and drop it in the empty space at the right of the detail section. Both a label and a text box appear in the space.

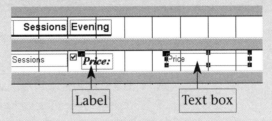

Figure 7.4 Price field dragged into the detail section of the report

4   Select the label. The label needs to be moved to the page header, but the text box needs to be left where it is. You can click on the black handle in the top left corner of the label to move it by itself within the detail section, but you will probably find that you cannot drag the label by itself to the page header. Instead, give the Cut command by clicking the Cut button on the toolbar. The label disappears but the text box should stay in place. Click into the page header section. Give the Paste command by clicking the Paste button on the toolbar. The label appears in the page header, but it is at the left-hand edge. Drag the label to the right until it is above its text box.

5   Move both the label and the text box closer to the Evening field. Make the text box smaller and line up its right-hand end with the right-hand end of the label.

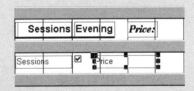

Figure 7.5 Price label and text box positioned in report

6   Switch to preview to see the effect of your changes, then switch back to design view.

7   Select the label of the Course code field and delete it using the delete key on the keyboard. Use the key labelled Delete, not the backspace delete key with the arrow.

8   Select the text box of the Course code field and delete that too.

9   Swap the positions of the Site and the Course name fields by dragging their labels and text boxes. Move the other fields to close up any big gaps. Keep checking in preview as you work to see the effect of your changes. Aim to have the fields arranged rather like Figure 7.6.

Course name	Site	Sessions	Evening	*Price:*
Introducing the Internet	Hilltop Centre	12	☑	£52.00
Starting MS Excel	Hilltop Centre	11	☐	£57.00
Starting MS Word	Hilltop Centre	10	☑	£52.00

Figure 7.6 Part of the report after moving fields

10   Save the report before you continue.

11   Change the format of the Price label so that it matches the other field name labels, and delete the colon (:).

12   The main part of the report would fit on paper in portrait orientation, but the page number text box in the page footer is too far to the right. Move the page number text box to the left until it is under the fields.

13   There is a grey line in the page footer. Select the line so that resize handles appear. Use the handle at the right-hand end of the line to make the line shorter until it is the same length as the blue line in the page header. Take care not to move the end of the line up or down or the line will be crooked.

14   The report itself is too wide. Point the mouse to the right-hand edge of the report, where the white background ends and the dark grey begins. The mouse pointer should change to a double-headed arrow. Drag the edge of the report to the left so that the report is just wide enough to show all its fields.

15   Preview the report.

16   Click on the File menu and select Page Setup from the drop down list. Click on the Page tab in the Page Setup dialogue box and select Portrait orientation. Click OK.

17   Close the preview and switch back to design view. Save the report before you continue.

Task 7.9   Add a total to a report

You will find the total number of sessions to be booked for courses shown in your rptSessions report.

Method

1   Start with your rptSessions report in design view.

2   Totals for the whole report need to go in the report footer. There is probably no space for a report footer yet. Point the mouse to the lower border of the grey bar labelled Report Footer and drag down to create a space.

3   Click on the Text box button in the toolbox **ab|**

4   Draw a rectangle in the report footer below the Sessions field text box. A text box and a label appear, with the label on the left. The label will display the word 'Text' followed by a number. The text box will display the word 'unbound'.

5   Edit your label to say **Total:**

6   In your new text box, key in a formula to add up the number of sessions: **=SUM([Sessions])**

7   Switch to preview. If all is well, the total number of sessions will appear after the last record of the report. If there are problems, go back and check that you have keyed in the formula correctly. It needs the = sign at the start. It needs the round brackets and the square brackets the right way round and in the right order.

8   Save your report in design view.

9   Preview again and print the report.

10 Close the report.

Information: Text boxes and the SUM function

Labels contain ordinary text. Text boxes are more interesting. They can be bound or unbound. A bound text box is linked to a field in a query or table and it displays data from that field. It can also be used to enter data into the field. You used bound text boxes for data entry on forms. There is a row of text boxes in the detail section of your report, and these are bound text boxes linked to fields. An unbound text box is not linked to a field. It has various uses, and one of these is to contain a formula to carry out a calculation. You have met a text box that contained the formula **=Now()** to find today's date.

If you have used a spreadsheet, you will know that the SUM function is used for adding up everything it finds in its round brackets. In a spreadsheet it is likely to find cell references, e.g. **=SUM(C4:C8)**. A database does not have cell references. Instead, you tell the SUM function which field values to add up. It must be a field that contains numbers. The square brackets round the field name tell Access that this is a field name. You can leave them out if the field name is one word, but you must include them if the field name has more than one word. It is safest to use the square brackets every time so that you are in the habit of using them. **=SUM([Sessions])** means that Access should add up all the values in the Sessions field and display the result when the report is previewed.

Task 7.10   Change the sorting order of a report

You will sort the records in your rptSessions report in order of price.

Method

1   Open your rptCourses report in design view.

2   Find and click the Sorting and Grouping button on the toolbar. The Sorting and Grouping window appears.

3   Click the arrow in the first column of the window and select Price from the drop down list of field names. Leave the sort order with the default value of Ascending. Select the Course name row by clicking in the grey area to its left, and delete it. There will be a message asking you to confirm the deletion. Click Yes.

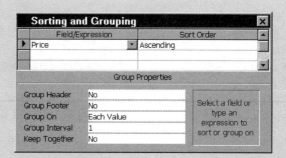

Figure 7.7 The Sorting and Grouping window

4   Close the Sorting and Grouping window by clicking its X button.
5   Save the report.
6   Switch to preview and check that the records are displayed in order of price.
7   Close the report.

Task 7.11 — Create a report with grouped data and subheadings

You will create a new report that groups courses by their site. You will find the number of sessions to be booked at each site.

Method

I   Create a new query based on the Courses table. Include all the fields. Do not put in any criteria. Save the query as **qryForRptSite**. Close the query.

2   In the reports section of your database window, double click on 'Create report by using wizard'.

3   In the first dialogue box of the wizard, select your qryForRptSite query from the list of tables and queries. Select all the fields for use in the report. Click Next.

4   In the second dialogue box you can choose grouping levels. Select Site from the list of fields on the left. Click the arrow pointing to the right. The display changes to show that report will group by Site. Click the Next button.

5   In the third dialogue box, select Course code in box I so that records will be sorted within their groups by Course code.

6   Click the Summary Options button. A new window opens in front of the wizard. Click in the Sum box of the Sessions row. Click OK.

Figure 7.8 Part of the Summary Options window

7   Click Next to move to the next wizard dialogue box.
8   Keep the stepped layout and portrait orientation. Click Next.
9   Keep the corporate style. Click Next.
10 Key in the title **rptSite** and click Finish.

11   The report should show the Hilltop Centre courses first, sorted by Course code. There should then be a summary for the group, showing the sum of the number of sessions. The Riverside courses come next, sorted by Course code. This group also has a summary showing the sum of the number of sessions. There is then a grand total showing the number of sessions at both sites. Some of the field names may not be fully displayed.

12   Switch to design view.

13   The report design has a new section called Site Header. This is the header area for the grouping. It contains a text box showing the field name 'Site' in design view. In preview there is a group header at the start of each group, and the text box displays the contents of the Site field, Hilltop Centre or Riverside. Switch to preview and back to see how this works.

14   There is another new section called Site Footer. This is the footer area for the group. It contains a long text box starting 'Summary for' and containing codes to show the field data and how many records there are. It also contains a label displaying 'Sum' and a text box with the familiar function =SUM([Sessions]). Switch to preview and see how this footer appears at the end of each group of records.

15   Look at the report footer to see the function =SUM([Sessions]) again. This time it is adding up all the values as it did when you keyed it in yourself in the previous report.

16   Edit the title to display '**Course Sessions at each site**'.

17   If any field names are not displaying fully, make their labels wider and adjust the spacing until they do show fully.

18   If the sum of sessions is not directly under the Sessions field, move it. Remember that numbers align to the right in their text boxes, so you need to line up the right-hand ends of the boxes.

19   Add your name in the page footer.

20   Save the design when you are satisfied.

Task 7.12   **Add an image to a report**

You will add an image to your rptSite report.

Method

1   Start with your rptSite report in design view.

2   Select the report header area by clicking in it.

3   Click on the Insert menu and select Object from the drop down list.

4   Select Microsoft Clip Gallery from the list in the Insert Object dialogue box. Click OK.

5   Choose a suitable piece of clipart and insert it.

6   Move the image to an empty area of the header. You will probably need to resize the frame round the clipart image. You will probably also need to change the Size Mode property to Zoom as you did for the image on the form. The property window is probably already visible. If not, you can show it by right clicking on the image and selecting Properties from the pop-up menu. As an alternative to clipart, you could use the toolbox to put in an Image, and find a suitable image file for it, as you did with the form. Use the method that is more convenient on your computer system.

7 Save the report.

8 Preview and print the report.

9 Close the report. Close down Access.

→ Practise your skills 7.1: Books database

You will create some queries based on your Books table, and then create reports based on the queries.

1 Open your Books database.

2 Create a query based on your Books table. Include all the fields. Put in a criteron to select records for books that are in stock. Save your query as **qryForRptBooks**.

3 Use the report wizard to create a report based on the qryForRptBooks query. Select the Author, Title, In Stock and Year Published fields and include them in the report. Do not put in any grouping. Sort in order of Author. Use tabular layout and portrait orientation. Use any style of your choice.

4 Give your report the name **rptBooks**.

5 In design view, edit the title to display '**Books**'. Adjust any field names that do not show in full. Add your name in the page footer.

6 Save the report. Print the report. Close the report.

7 Use your report to print a list of books that cost less than £10. Include books that are out of stock as well as books that are in stock. (**Hint:** Change the criteria in the query but do not make any changes to the report design.)

8 Create a query based on your Books table. Include all the fields. Do not put in any criteria. Save your query as **qryForRptAuthor**.

9 Use the report wizard to create a report based on the qryForRptAuthor query. Include all the fields in the report. Group by Author. Sort in order of Title within the groups. In the Summary Options, select the sum of Price. Use a stepped layout and any style of your choice. Call your report **rptAuthor**.

10 In design view, change the title of the report to display '**Books grouped by Author**'. Adjust field names if necessary so that they show in full. Add your name in the page footer.

11 Save the report. Print the report. Close the report.

12 Open the rptBooks report in design view.

13 Delete the Year Published field. Add the Price field. Make any necessary formatting changes so that your new field matches the others.

14 Sort the records in ascending order of Price.

15 Add a suitable image in the report header.

16 Save the report. Print the report. Close the report.

17 Close down Access.

→ Practise your skills 7.2: Seeds database

You are asked to create and print some reports based on your Seeds table. Create a query first for each report so that you are able to select the records to display. The formatting and other detail may not be specified. Choose suitable formatting of your own and make each report look as good as possible. Make sure that all field names and data show in full. Each report should show your name in a footer. Choose suitable names for all queries and reports.

1 Open your Seeds database.
2 Create a columnar report showing the name, price and height of flower varieties that flower in June. Sort the records in order of Height.
3 Print the report and write Printout 1 on the printout.
4 Add the CatNo and Flowering Date fields to your columnar report. Sort in order of CatNo. Use the report to show all the records for seeds that are available.
5 Print the report and write Printout 2 on the printout.
6 Create a tabular report showing all the fields. Sort in order of Name. Put a suitable image in the report header. Use your report to display records of varieties with a height of 50 cm or less.
7 Print the report and write Printout 3 on the printout.
8 Delete the Available field from your tabular report. Use the report to display records of varieties that are available and that flower in July. A customer wants to know the cost of buying one packet of seed of each of these varieties, so find the total of the Price field.
9 Print the report and write Printout 4 on the printout.
10 Create a new report showing all the fields. Group by Flowering Date and sort by CatNo. Find the sum of the Price for each group. Use landscape orientation. Use your report to show all the records.
12 Print the report and write Printout 5 on the printout.
13 Close down Access.

Hint:

You can show a £ sign in the total. Select the text box containing the function that finds the total. In its properties window, find the Format property and select Currency from its drop down list.

→ Check your knowledge

1 What is the normal use of a report?
2 Why can it be an advantage to base a report on a query and not on a table?
3 What is the advantage of using the report wizard rather than an autoreport?
4 You want to put your name in a report footer. Should you use a label or a text box?
5 A report has a Cost field containing currency values. You want to put the total of these values in a footer. Should you use a label or a text box?
6 What formula should you key into your label or text box to find the total cost?

You are asked to create a database for Hodgkins Estate Agents. They have branches in Rencaster and Tadfield. The database will hold information about houses for sale. You will create queries, forms and reports. You will make some changes, and export a table.

1 On paper, design a table to be used to store the data shown in Table 7.1. List the field names, the data types and the field size and/or format. Decide on a suitable primary key and write down its name.

House ID	Owner	Location	Bedrooms	Price	Date on market	Description
2001	Jowett	Rencaster	3	£109,995.00	06/02/03	semi, garden
2002	Chadworth	Renford	3	£149,995.00	06/02/03	det, garage, garden
2003	Debney	Renford	4	£169,995.00	07/02/03	det, garden, garage
2004	Hoskins	Rencaster	2	£99,995.00	11/02/03	terr, garden
2005	Brown	Rencaster	4	£149,995.00	11/02/03	semi, garden
2006	Lipton	Renford	3	£139,995.00	13/02/03	det, garage, garden

Table 7.1 Data for the Houses table in the Rencaster database

2 Create a new Access database called **Rencaster**. Create a table called **Houses** according to your design. Set the primary key.

3 Use the documenter to print out the table design. Write PRINTOUT 1 on the print out.

4 Enter the data from Table 7.1 into your Database table.

5 Print your table on one sheet of paper. This is PRINTOUT 2.

6 Create another new Access database called **Tadfield**.

7 Export the structure only of your Houses table from the Rencaster database to the Tadfield database. Keep the name **Houses** for your new table. Check that the Tadfield database now contains a table called Houses with the same structure as the original table, but containing no records.

8 Create a data entry form for the Houses table in the Tadfield database. It should be in columnar layout, and it should have a heading: **Hodgkins Estate Agents**. Save the form as **frmHouses**.

9 Use your data entry form to enter the following data as shown in Table 7.2.

House ID	Owner	Location	Bedrooms	Price	Date on market	Description
3001	Drew	Tadfield	4	£138,995.00	15/01/03	det, garage, garden
3002	Shah	Tadfield	4	£137,995.00	21/01/03	det, garden, garage
3003	Kane	Tadfield	3	£122,995.00	22/01/03	terr, garden
3004	Prentice	Tadmouth	2	£109,995.00	11/02/03	semi, garden
3005	Tang	Tadfield	3	£122,995.00	11/02/03	det, garden, garage
3006	Thompson	Tadmouth	3	£119,995.00	13/02/03	semi, garage, garden

Table 7.2 Data for the Houses table in the Tadfield database

10 Display the record for the house owned by Kane, and print the form showing this record only. This is PRINTOUT 3.

11 Create an index on the Houses table in the Tadfield database. Use Bedrooms as the primary sort field and Location as the secondary sort field. Sort the table on Bedrooms and on Location within Bedrooms.

12 Print the table on one sheet of paper. This is PRINTOUT 4.

13 Return to the Rencaster database. Select all houses in Renford and append them to the Houses table in the Tadfield database. Use an append query, or you could use an ordinary select query then copy and paste.

14 Print the Houses table from the Tadfield database, sorted by Bedrooms and Location as before, on one sheet of paper. This is PRINTOUT 5.

15 From now on, use the Tadfield database. Modify the design of the Houses table by adding an extra field. The field name is **Sold** and the data type is Logical (Yes/No).

16 Modify the data input form by adding the extra field.

17 Print a screenshot showing the form with the extra field. This is PRINTOUT 6.

18 Create a query to show houses with 3 bedrooms and a garage. Save the query as **qry3garage**.

19 Create a tabular report based on this query. It should show the House ID, Location, Price and Description fields only, displayed in that order. The records should be sorted by price. Save the report as **rpt3garage**. Give the report a heading **Hodgkins Estate Agents** and a subheading **3-bed houses with garage**. Add an appropriate image next to the heading.

20 Print the report. This is PRINTOUT 7.

21 Create a tabular report to show all records. It should show all fields, grouped on Location and sorted on Date on market. Show the total price for each group, and the total Price for all the records. The font for fields and totals should be size 10. Space out fields if necessary, and make sure that all totals are shown in full. The heading should be **Totals from Sales of Houses**.

22 Print the report. This is PRINTOUT 8.

23 Close Access.

You will learn to

- Paste a screen shot into MS Word and print it out
- Paste data from an Access table into a table in MS Word
- Paste data from a table in MS Word to an Access table
- Paste data from an Access table to an Excel worksheet
- Paste data from an Excel worksheet to an Access table
- Export an Access report to Word using an .rtf file
- Export an Access table to an Excel worksheet
- Import an Excel worksheet into an Access table
- Import a .csv text file into an Access table

Information: Screen shots

It is possible to capture the image that is displayed on the screen and put it on the clipboard. The image can then be pasted into any kind of file that is able to handle images. It can be printed and it can be saved as part of the file. This method of taking screen shots can provide useful additional evidence to show that you are working correctly. You may be asked to produce screen shots as part of the Level 2 test.

In this section you will learn how to make a screen shot and paste it into a Microsoft Word document. Alternatively, you could paste your screen shots into a document created using Paint, Wordpad, Microsoft Publisher, or any other application that can manage images.

Before starting the tasks, you need to be able to use Microsoft Word to create a document, key in text, save and print a document.

Hint:

Screen shots are sometimes called screen dumps.

Task 8.1 | Paste a screen shot into MS Word and print it out

You will print out a screen shot showing the design view of a query.

Method

1. Open your Courses table and open your qryRiverside query in design view. If you do not have this query then you can use another query.
2. Find the Print Screen (or PrnScr) key on your keyboard. This is normally in the top row to the right of the function keys, in a little group of nine keys. Some keyboards have the key a little lower down, to the right of the Backspace Delete key. The key may be labelled Print Screen/SysRq.
3. Press the Print Screen key. Nothing seems to happen, but an image of the screen is placed on the clipboard.

If you use the Print Screen key by itself, it will capture an image of the whole screen and put it on the clipboard. If you hold down the Alt key as you press Print Screen, it will capture only your selected window.

Hint:

You can paste your screen shot into Paint or another graphics package. You can then select a small part of it to paste into Word.

4   Start up Microsoft Word. A new empty document should be created.
5   Key in **Design of qryRiverside query**. Press the Enter key to move to the next line.
6   Give the Paste command. You can use the toolbar Paste button or you can select Paste from the Edit menu or you can use the keyboard shortcut Ctrl+v.
7   An image of the screen, including the query design window, should be pasted into your Word document.
8   Save the Word document and print it. You could use this as evidence that you created the query correctly.

Information: Integrated applications

Access is part of the Microsoft Office package, and it is designed to work closely with other applications within Microsoft Office. You will learn how to copy data between Access and other applications. The remainder of this section will be of particular interest to anyone who is planning to take the City & Guilds e-Quals Level 2 Integrated Applications unit. It is not essential for the Databases Level 2 unit, but the skills introduced here are useful for everyday work. If time is short, you could move on to the practice assignments, then complete this section after taking the real assignment.

Most applications that run under the Windows operating system will allow some degree of transfer of data using copy and paste. Some can integrate better than others. Possibilities include the following:

- You paste data into a file, and it behaves as if it had been entered into that file in the first place. It can be edited and formatted just like any other data in the file. There is no link between the pasted data and the original data. If you change one, the other is not affected.
- You paste data into a file. It does not behave like data that was created in the file, but you can select it, double click to bring up its original application, and edit it that way. There is no link between the pasted data and the original data. If you change one, the other is not affected. The data is said to be **embedded** in its new file.
- You paste data into a file. The data itself is not copied into the file, but it makes a link with the original data. You can see the data displayed in the file. You can select it, double click to bring up its original application, and edit it. You are editing the data in the original file. The data is **linked**.
- You paste data into a file. The data is displayed as an image that cannot be edited or formatted.

By default, copy and paste will give you the best integration that Windows can manage for the particular type of data you are copying, and the applications you are using.

For some of the following exercises you need to create a table in Word. There are some exercises on copying between Access and Excel that need a basic knowledge of Excel.

<table>
<tr><td>Task 8.2</td><td>Paste data from an Access table into a table in MS Word</td></tr>
</table>

You can prepare a document using Word, and paste in a table of data from an Access table.

Method

1   Use your Courses database again, and open the Courses table so that you can see the data.
2   Select all the rows of the table, and give the Copy command.
3   Open a new Word document. Key in: **The following courses are running**. Press Enter twice to leave a clear line.
4   Give the Paste command.
5   The data from the Access table should appear, complete with field names at the top of the columns. The data is now in a Word table. You can edit and format the data and the table just as if you had created the table in Word.
6   Try editing the data. If you have learned about Word tables then you can try altering the table layout or formatting. Save and print your Word document.
7   Close down Access. When you have copied data from one application to another, you may see a message when you close an application.

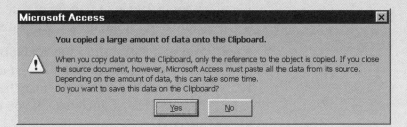

Figure 8.1 Warning message on copying data

If you have finished pasting the data and do not need to keep it on the clipboard any longer, then click No. If you need the data again, then click Yes to keep it on the clipboard after the application has closed.

<table>
<tr><td>Task 8.3</td><td>Paste data from a table in MS Word to an Access table</td></tr>
</table>

It is possible, with care, to copy data from a Word table into Access. The data must be of a suitable type for the field it is pasted into, and must obey any rules that have been set up in the table.

Method

1   Start MS Word and create a table in a new document as shown in Table 8.1.

C711	Introducing Outlook	Mayhill	5	09-Sep-02	£40.00	Yes
C721	Mastering Outlook	Mayhill	5	02-Nov-02	£40.00	No
C731	Advanced Outlook	Riverside	5	08-Jan-03	£50.00	No

Table 8.1 A table created in Word

2   Select all three rows of the table. Give the Copy command.
3   Open the Courses table of your Courses database.
4   Select the whole of the empty row at the bottom of the table. Give the Paste command.
5   You should see the three records appear, with a message that they are about to be pasted in. Click Yes.
6   Close the table. Close Access and close Word.

Hint:

Short sections of normal text can be pasted into individual fields of a table.

Task 8.4 — Paste data from an Access table to an Excel worksheet

You can copy and paste from Access to Excel, though there are alternative methods to be described later.

Method

1   Open the Courses table of your Courses database.
2   Select all the records and give the Copy command.
3   Start Excel so that you have a new empty worksheet.
4   Give the Paste command.
5   The records and the field names appear in the worksheet. You may need to adjust column widths and other formatting.
6   Save your spreadsheet file as **Courses Pasted.xls** and close Excel.

Task 8.5 — Paste data from an Excel worksheet to an Access table

With care, you can copy and paste from Excel to Access. The data must be of a suitable type for the field it is pasted into, and must obey any rules that have been set up in the table.

Method

1   Enter the following data into an Excel worksheet.

| C811 | Visual Basic 1 | Riverside | 20 | 15-Sep-02 | £120.00 | TRUE |
| C812 | Visual Basic 2 | Riverside | 30 | 16-Sep-02 | £200.00 | TRUE |

Table 8.2 Data for an Excel worksheet

2 Select all 14 cells and give the Copy command.

3 Open the Courses table of your Courses database.

4 Select the whole of the empty bottom row of the table.

5 Give the Paste command. The two rows should be pasted in. Reply Yes to the message.

Information: Exporting and importing data

Access provides export and import facilities which are sometimes more useful than copy and paste. You have already used the export method to copy a table or a table structure to a different database file. You can export tables, queries, forms and reports to a variety of different types of file. You can also import data to Access from files of different types.

Task 8.6 | Export an Access report to Word using an .rtf file

It can be useful to have a report in a form that can be edited in Word, or sent by e-mail.

Method

1 Open the rptCourses report from your Courses database, so that you can see the data in preview.

2 Click on the File menu and select Export. The Export dialogue box appears.

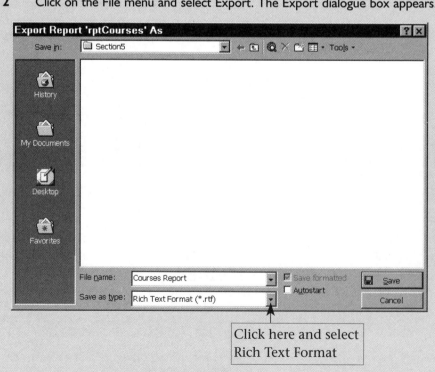

Click here and select Rich Text Format

Figure 8.2 The Export Report dialogue box

3	Find the box labelled 'Save as type'. Click the arrow on the right to show the list of options. Scroll down and select Rich Text Format.
4	Choose where you want to save the file, and give it a suitable name.
5	Click Save.
6	Close Access.
7	Open your Rich Text Format file. You can do this using Word. Your report can be freely edited. You can copy parts of it if you wish. You could attach it to an e-mail. There is only one problem. The data in the Logical field is not shown. You would need to alter the original report to display the data as TRUE and FALSE instead of check boxes in order to make the data display in your .rtf file.
8	Close your file.

Task 8.7	Export an Access table to an Excel worksheet

Exporting data from an Access table to an Excel worksheet gives a similar result to the copy and paste method that you used earlier.

Method

1	Open your Courses database. Select the Courses table but do not open it.
2	Click on the File menu and select Export from the list. The Export dialogue box appears.
3	Show the 'Save as type' drop down list and select 'Microsoft Excel 97-2000'. Choose the folder where you want to save the spreadsheet file. Change the file name to **Courses Spreadsheet**. Click Save.
4	Close Access.
5	Open the Courses Spreadsheet file. The data from the table is in the spreadsheet, complete with its field names. You may need to adjust cell widths.
6	Close the file and close Excel.

Hint:

You could repeat Task 8.7, but select the check box labelled 'Formatted' before clicking Save at the end of step 3. Formatting from the database table is copied to the spreadsheet.

Task 8.8	Import an Excel worksheet into an Access table

When you create an Access table, you normally create it in design view, setting up field names, data types, etc. When you import data to create an Access table, there is a wizard to help you set up the design of the table to suit the data.

Method

1. Start up Excel and key the following data into a spreadsheet. Save the spreadsheet in the same folder as your Courses database and give it the name **Gardening.xls**.

	A	B	C	D	E	F	G
1	Course code	Course name	Site	Sessions	Start date	Price	Evening
2	D223	Garden design 1	Riverside	10	16/09/02	£ 50.00	Yes
3	D224	Garden design 2	Riverside	10	06/01/03	£ 50.00	Yes
4	D225	Advanced gardens	Hilltop Centre	30	17/09/02	£200.00	Yes

Table 8.3 Data for the Gardening worksheet

2. Close Excel.
3. Open your Courses database.
4. Click on the File menu and select 'Get External Data', then select 'Import'. The Import dialogue box appears.
5. Use the 'Files of Type' drop down list and choose 'Microsoft Excel'. Find and select your Gardening.xls file. Click Import.
6. The Import Spreadsheet wizard runs. In the first step, you can choose a worksheet or range. Your data should already be selected so that there are no changes to make. Click Next.
7. In the second step, you specify whether or not the first row of data contains column headings. In this case it does, and the check box should be ticked. Click Next.
8. In the third step you can choose to store your data in a new table or in an existing table. Choose a new table and click Next.
9. In the fourth step you can make some decisions about the properties of each field, though your choices are limited by the kind of data in each field. You can change the field name, or you can decide not to import a field. You can set indexes. Click into each field in turn to see the data types and properties that are being set, but do not make any changes. Click Next.
10. In the fifth step you can choose a primary key or let Access add an extra primary key field. Choose your own primary key, and select Course code. Click Next.
11. In the final step you provide a name for the table. Call it **Gardening Courses**. Click Finish.
12. There should be a message to confirm that the import has taken place. Click OK.
13. Open the Gardening Courses table. Inspect it in datasheet view and in design view.
14. Text fields are set to the maximum size of 255 characters. Change the sizes to something more appropriate. You could also change the Evening field to the Yes/No data type. Save the altered table design.
15. Close the table and close Access.

Task 8.9	Import a .csv text file into an Access table

A comma separated values (.csv) file is a plain text file containing data items separated by commas. Data stored in this format can be imported into a variety of applications.

Method

1   Start Notepad. This can usually be found from the Start menu by choosing Programs, Applications. Notepad is a simple text editor.

2   Key in the following text into Notepad. Be careful to include commas exactly as shown.

```
Course code,Course name,Site,Sessions,Start date,Price,Evening
E332,Flower painting,Hilltop Centre,10,26/9/2002,52.00,Yes
E405,Life class,Riverside,11,27/9/2002,52.00,No
```

3   Save the file with the name **Art** as a text file. Close Notepad.

4   Open the Courses database.

5   Click on the File menu and select 'Get External Data', then select 'Import'. The Import dialogue box appears.

6   Use the 'Files of Type' drop down list and choose 'Text files (*.txt;*.csv;*.tab;*.asc)'. Find and select your Art.txt file. Click Import.

7   The Import Text wizard runs. In the first step, you can choose delimited or fixed width fields. Keep delimited fields. Click Next.

8   In the second step, you choose the type of delimiter. Comma should be selected. You also specify whether or not the first row of data contains column headings. In this case it does, and the check box should be ticked. Click Next.

9   In the third step, choose to save the data in a new table.

10   In the fourth step you can adjust the choice of data types for the fields. Change the Price field data type to Currency. Change the Evening field data type to Yes/No. Click Next.

11   In the fifth step, choose your own primary key, and make it Course code. Click Next.

12   In the final step, give the new table the name **Art Courses**. Click Finish.

13   There should be a message to confirm that the import has taken place. Click OK.

14   Open the Art Courses table. Inspect it in datasheet view and in design view.

15   Change the sizes of the text fields from 255 to something more appropriate. Change the format of the Evening field to True/False so that it does not display 0 and −1. Save the altered table design.

16   Close the table and close Access.

Hint:

You may see an error message in step 13, saying that there was a problem in setting the primary key. This happens if there were empty rows at the end of your text file. Your table can still be created, but the primary key will not be set. You can delete any empty rows from your table, then set the primary key yourself.

An Access table can be exported in the form of a .csv file. You could try this out for yourself. Start by selecting the Courses table as you did in Task 8.7. Select Export from the File menu and run the Export wizard. The file type to choose is 'Text files (*.txt;*.csv;*.tab;*.asc)'. Follow the wizard. You should be able to open your .csv file in either Notepad or in Excel.

This use of a .csv file is valuable if you want to transfer data between applications that are not well integrated, such as incompatible database packages.

Practice assignments

You will take one assignment in order to complete your City & Guilds Databases Level 2 qualification. Pass, Credit and Distinction grades are available. Two practice assignments are available here. Your tutor will give you the real assignment when you are ready.

Practice assignment 1: Glazing

Candidates are advised to read all instructions carefully before starting work and to check with your assessor, if necessary, to ensure that you have fully understood what is required.

You must, at all times, observe all relevant health and safety precautions.

Time allowed 4 hours

Introduction

This assignment is broken down into seven parts:

1 A brief scenario is provided for candidates.
2 Task A requires you to design a database structure on paper, implement that design, create a data input form and enter records into the database.
3 Task B requires you to modify the database structure, modify a form, enter additional data and sort records.
4 Task C requires you to copy the database structure from an existing database to a new database, select existing records and enter them into the new database.
5 Task D requires you to edit the contents of selected fields and create queries for a table.
6 Task E requires you to produce reports based on tables and previously created queries.
7 Task F requires you to backup a database.

> **Scenario**
> You work for Westwind Windows. This company sells replacement windows and doors. You have been asked to design, implement and maintain a database of customers. You are asked to include the following information about each customer:
> - Lastname
> - Initials
> - Street (and house number)
> - Town
> - County
> - Amount of order
> - Date of order
> - Paid or not
> - Sale number

Task A

In this task you are required to design a database structure on paper, implement that design, create a data input form and enter records into the database.

1. Create two new directories on disk and name them GLAZING and GLAZINGBU.
2. On paper, design the database table structure to store the information supplied in Figure 9.1 at the end of this assignment. Show the field names, data types and field sizes. Label the document DESIGN.
3. Select one field where no duplicates would apply as the primary key. On the paper design, show which field is to be used as the primary key.
4. Open the database application software to create a new database.
5. The table is to be saved as CUSTOMER and the database as GLAZINGDB. The database is to be saved to the directory GLAZING.
6. Implement your design and create the CUSTOMER table.
7. Create a data entry form to enter the data into the CUSTOMER table. Name this form FRMCUSTOMER. Give it a heading 'Customer Details'.
8. Use the data entry form to enter the first record from Figure 9.1. Print the form showing this record and label it PRINTOUT 1.
9. Enter the remaining customer records shown in Figure 9.1 into the CUSTOMER table.
10. Print a copy of the database structure for CUSTOMER and label it PRINTOUT 2.
11. Print out all of the records from the CUSTOMER table in landscape mode. Label it PRINTOUT 3.

Task B

In this task you are required to modify the database structure, modify a form, enter additional data and sort records.

1. In the CUSTOMER table, add a field after the Lastname field and call it Title. This should be a Text field of length 5.
2. In the CUSTOMER table, add a field after the DateOrdered field and call it DateInstalled. Give the field a suitable data type.
3. Modify the data entry form to include the new fields.
4. Add the data for the new fields as shown in Figure 9.2.
5. Add new customers as shown in Figure 9.3.
6. Sort the records into ascending order of DateInstalled. Print out a copy of the sorted records in landscape and label it PRINTOUT 4.

Task C

In this task you are required to copy the database structure from an existing database to a new database, add new records, select existing records and enter them into the new database.

1. Create a new database, name it OXFORDSHIREDB and save it in the GLAZING directory.
2. Copy the database structure definition only for the CUSTOMER table in the GLAZINGDB to a new table named TBLSALES in the OXFORDSHIREDB.

3 Create a query from the CUSTOMER table in the GLAZINGDB to show all fields for customers who live in Oxfordshire. Name the query QRYOXFORDSHIRE.
4 Screen print the query design and label it PRINTOUT 5.
5 Run the query and copy the resulting records into the new table TBLSALES in the OXFORDSHIREDB.
6 Print the contents of the table TBLSALES in order of sale number, in landscape, and label it PRINTOUT 6.

Task D

In this task you are required to edit the contents of selected fields and create queries for the CUSTOMER table in the database GLAZINGDB.

1 Close the database OXFORDSHIREDB.
2 In the CUSTOMER table of the GLAZINGDB database, for the County field, use Find and Replace to change the word Berkshire to West Berkshire.
3 Print the table contents in landscape showing the change and sorted by SaleNumber. Label it PRINTOUT 7.
4 Create a query to show SaleNumber, Lastname, Amount and DateInstalled for those customers who have not yet paid. Save the query as QRYUNPAID. (No need to print.)
5 Create a query to show Lastname, Title, Initials, DateOrdered and DateInstalled for customers who live in Abingdon and who ordered on or after 04/03/02. Save the query as QRYABINGDONRECENT.
6 Create a query to show all fields for customers who live in Oxfordshire and who have already paid an amount greater than £250. Save the query as QRYOXFORDSHIREPAID.
7 Create a query to show all fields for customers whose amount is over £500 or whose installation date is after 01/04/02. Save the query as QRYAMOUNTDATE. Close the GLAZINGDB database.

Task E

In this task you are required to produce reports based on tables and previously created queries.

1 Open the database OXFORDSHIREDB. Create a report in landscape that shows all fields and all records in the table TBLSALES in the database OXFORDSHIREDB. Sort by Lastname. Give the report the heading 'Oxfordshire Sales'. Place a header on the form showing your name and a footer showing the date, PRINTOUT 8 and the page number. Save the report in the OXFORDSHIREDB as RPTSALES and print the report. There may be more than one page.
2 Close the OXFORDSHIREDB and open the GLAZINGDB.
3 Create a report based on the query QRYUNPAID to include the fields for SaleNumber, Lastname, Amount and DateInstalled in that order. Sort by DateInstalled. Give the report a title 'Payments due'. Place a header on the report form showing your name and a footer showing the date, PRINTOUT 9 and the page number. Save the report in the GLAZINGDB as RPTUNPAID and print the report.
4 Create a report based on the query QRYABINGDONRECENT to include the fields for Lastname, Title, Initials, DateOrdered and DateInstalled.

Sort by Lastname. Give the report a title 'Abingdon orders on or after 04/03/02'. Place a header on the form showing your name and a footer showing the date, PRINTOUT 10 and the page number. Save the report in the GLAZINGDB as RPTABINGDONRECENT and print the report.

5 Create a report in landscape based on the query QRYAMOUNTDATE to include the fields for Sale Number, Amount, Paid, DateOrdered, DateInstalled, Lastname, Title, Initials, Address, Town, and County in that order. Sort by SaleNumber. Give the report the title 'Orders over £500 or recently installed'. Place a header on the form showing your name and a footer showing the date, PRINTOUT 11 and the page number. Widen or move labels or fields if necessary to ensure that all labels and data are fully displayed. Save the report in the GLAZINGDB as RPTAMOUNTDATE and print the report.

6 Create a report based on the query QRYOXFORDSHIREPAID to include the fields for Lastname, Title, Initials, Address, Town, and Amount in that order. Sort by Amount. Give the report a title 'Oxfordshire customers who have paid'. Place a header on the form showing your name and a footer showing the date, PRINTOUT 12 and the page number. Save the report in the GLAZINGDB as RPTOXFORDSHIREPAID and print the report.

7 Delete the Title field from the RPTOXFORDSHIREPAID report. Move your name to the footer. Add an image in the header. Field names and fields should have font size 10. Show the total amount paid. Adjust the footer to show PRINTOUT 13. Save the altered report and print it.

8 Close the database application.

Task F

In this task you are required to back up the databases.

1 Copy GLAZINGDB and OXFORDSHIREDB into the directory GLAZINGBU.

Note
- At the conclusion of this assignment, hand all paperwork and disks to the test supervisor.
- Ensure that your name is on the disk (if using a floppy disk) and all documentation.
- If the assignment is taken over more than one period, all floppy disks and paperwork must be returned to the test supervisor at the end of each sitting.

Lastname	Initials	Address	Town	County	Amount	Paid	DateOrdered	SaleNumber
Baley	D	4 Windrush Way	Abingdon	Oxfordshire	412.00	Yes	12/12/01	106
Nelson	G	9 Akenham Close	Abingdon	Oxfordshire	525.50	Yes	15/12/01	107
Goldman	S	3 Harrison Close	Didcot	Oxfordshire	602.28	Yes	03/01/02	108
Patel	S	12 Sewell Close	Abingdon	Oxfordshire	409.95	Yes	05/01/02	109
McPherson	M	45 Long Lane	Wantage	Oxfordshire	220.65	Yes	08/01/02	110
Draycott	F	7 Hollow Way	Wantage	Oxfordshire	378.50	Yes	16/01/02	111
Kimball	J	14 Frith Avenue	Didcot	Oxfordshire	380.25	Yes	23/01/02	112
Cunningham	H	63 Madison Gardens	Abingdon	Oxfordshire	309.45	Yes	12/02/02	113
Sutherland	N	12 Yarrow Drive	Abingdon	Oxfordshire	299.99	Yes	22/02/02	114
O'Neill	K	19 Jukes Walk	Didcot	Oxfordshire	770.50	Yes	23/02/02	115
Varju	S	102 Cowley Road	Oxford	Oxfordshire	210.50	Yes	25/02/02	116
Harley	D G	34 Towns Road	Oxford	Oxfordshire	445.20	Yes	25/02/02	117
Greenham	K	16 Cardigan Road	Abingdon	Oxfordshire	759.50	Yes	26/02/02	118
Farley	F R	15 Hookes Drive	Abingdon	Oxfordshire	385.20	Yes	26/02/02	119
Murphy	S	17 Harkman Close	Didcot	Oxfordshire	555.00	Yes	26/02/02	120
Ali	J	29 Woodland Road	Wantage	Oxfordshire	752.60	Yes	27/02/02	121
Perkins	P N	2 Somerset Drive	Newbury	Berkshire	953.00	Yes	28/02/02	122
Cordwainer	C	22 Ratcliffe Close	Didcot	Oxfordshire	547.30	Yes	28/02/02	123
Patel	S	12 Sewell Close	Abingdon	Oxfordshire	102.40	Yes	04/03/02	124
Hussein	S G	20 Marlborough Street	Newbury	Berkshire	457.60	Yes	08/03/02	125
Harrison	N E	22 Marlborough Street	Newbury	Berkshire	109.40	Yes	08/03/02	126
Goldman	S	3 Harrison Close	Didcot	Oxfordshire	605.90	No	09/03/02	127
Saunders	C	25 Cardigan Road	Abingdon	Oxfordshire	209.70	No	10/03/02	128
Teoh	O	16 Yarrow Drive	Abingdon	Oxfordshire	336.50	Yes	10/03/02	129
Smith	F R	6 Eastern Avenue	Didcot	Oxfordshire	709.20	No	15/03/02	130
Ling	J	1 Shelley Close	Newbury	Berkshire	886.30	No	15/03/02	131
Anders	J	6 Green Crescent	Newbury	Berkshire	858.10	Yes	16/03/02	132
Brown	S	19 Yarrow Drive	Abingdon	Oxfordshire	105.00	No	18/03/02	133
Solomon	K	42 Hendred Close	Wantage	Oxfordshire	650.00	No	18/03/02	134

Figure 9.1 Data for Customer table

Lastname	Title	DateInstalled	Sale_Number
Baley	Mr	04/01/02	106
Nelson	Mr	07/01/02	107
Goldman	Mr	21/01/02	108
Patel	Mr	22/01/02	109
McPherson	Mr	23/01/02	110
Draycott	Mr	28/01/02	111
Kimball	Ms	04/02/02	112
Cunningham	Mrs	25/02/02	113
Sutherland	Ms	04/03/02	114
O'Neill	Ms	05/03/02	115
Varju	Mr	06/03/02	116
Harley	Mr	07/03/02	117
Greenham	Ms	11/03/02	118
Farley	Mr	12/03/02	119
Murphy	Mr	13/03/02	120
Ali	Mr	16/04/02	121
Perkins	Mr	25/03/02	122
Cordwainer	Mr	26/03/02	123
Patel	Mr	17/04/02	124
Hussein	Mr	27/03/02	125
Harrison	Mr	18/04/02	126
Goldman	Mr	02/04/02	127
Saunders	Ms	15/04/02	128
Teoh	Mr	23/04/02	129
Smith	Mr	30/04/02	130
Ling	Mr	22/04/02	131
Anders	Mr	29/04/02	132
Brown	Mr	24/04/02	133
Solomon	Mr	01/05/02	134

Figure 9.2 Additional data for Customer table

Lastname	Title	Initials	Address	Town	County	Amount	Paid	Date Ordered	Date Installed	Sale Number
Grey	Ms	D	24 Marlborough Street	Newbury	Berkshire	510.50	No	22/03/02	02/05/02	135
Pauling	Mr	P	25 Sewell Close	Abingdon	Oxfordshire	220.00	No	22/03/02	03/05/02	136

Figure 9.3 Additional customers

Practice assignment 2: Vets

Candidates are advised to read all instructions carefully before starting work and to check with your assessor, if necessary, to ensure that you have fully understood what is required.

You must, at all times, observe all relevant health and safety precautions.

Time allowed 4 hours

Introduction

This assignment is broken down into six parts:

1 A brief scenario is provided for candidates.
2 Task A requires candidates to create a database, enter records and modify the database structure.
3 Task B requires candidates to copy the database structure to a new database, select records from the existing database and copy them to the new database and edit records.
4 Task C requires candidates to create a data entry form and add and edit a record using the form.
5 Task D requires candidates to create and run queries.
6 Task E requires candidates to create a report based on a query.

> **Scenario**
> You are employed to work in the office at Castlewell Vets. This is a vets' practice owned by four partners. One of your jobs is to maintain and improve a small database that was created to keep track of the small animals that are brought in for treatment.

Task A

In this task you are required to create a new database, enter records into the database and modify the database structure.

1 Create two new directories and name them VETS and VETSBACKUP.
2 Open the database application software.
3 Create a new database called VETSDB and save it in the directory called VETS.
4 Create a database structure for a SMALLANIMALS table including a primary key using the information in Figure 9.4. Write down the field names, data types and field sizes first. Write down the name of a suitable primary key field. Then create the table.
5 Enter the records shown in Figure 9.4 into the SMALLANIMALS table.
6 Print a copy of the database structure. Label this PRINTOUT1.
7 Print out all the records in the SMALLANIMALS table. Label this PRINTOUT2.
8 Modify the database structure as follows:
   a Delete the field showing the animal's sex.
   b Add a field called DATE BORN between the Name and the Type fields. Choose a suitable data type.

9   Print a copy of the database structure. Label this PRINTOUT3.
10 Add the data shown in Figure 9.5 to the DATE BORN field.
11 Print out all the data in the SMALLANIMALS table in landscape mode. Label this PRINTOUT4.
12 Close the VETSDB database and then copy it into the VETSBACKUP directory. Rename the file in the VETSBACKUP directory to clearly identify it as a backup file. Do a screen print to show the file in the VETSBACKUP directory. Label this SCREENPRINT1.

Task B

In this task you are required to copy the database structure from the existing database to a new database. You will then copy selected records from the existing database into the database and edit some records.

1   Create a new database, name it CASTLEWELLVETS and save it in the VETS directory.
2   Copy the database structure definition only for the SMALLANIMALS table in the VETSDB to a new table named DOGS in the CASTLEWELLVETS database.
3   Add the records shown in Figure 9.6 to the DOGS table.
4   Create a query on the SMALLANIMALS table in the VETSDB to select all the fields and find all the records for dogs. Name this query QRYDOGS.
5   Copy the records in the query QRYDOGS and append them to the DOGS table in the CASTLEWELLVETS database. Close the VETSDB database.
6   Print a copy of all the records in the DOGS table in landscape. Label this PRINTOUT5.
7   Select the records in the DOGS table where the dog was last treated before 01/07/02 and where the bill is paid up. Delete these records.
8   Mr Carew is retiring from the practice and is being replaced by Mr Duncan. Use Find and Replace to find all the occurrences of Carew and change them to Duncan.
9   Sort the DOGS table in ascending order of the DATE BORN field. Print out all the data in the DOGS table in landscape mode. Label this PRINTOUT6.

Task C

In this task you are required to create a data entry form for records in the DOGS table, add a new record and edit a record using the data entry form.

1   Design and create a data entry form for records in the DOGS table and name it FRMDOGS. Add the heading 'DOGS INPUT FORM' and centre it.
2   Enter the record shown in Figure 9.7. Print the input form to show only this record. Label this PRINTOUT7.
3   The owner's name for the dog with Patient_ID number 140 is incorrect. Use the data entry form to change the owner's name to Wilkins U. Print the input form to show this record. Label this PRINTOUT8.

Task D

In this task you are required to create and run queries on the CASTLEWELLVETS database.

1. Create a query to show all the fields to find all dogs last treated between 01/08/02 and 12/11/02 (inclusive). Sort in order of date last treated. Name the query QRYTREATED.
2. Print a copy of the results of the query QRYTREATED in landscape. Label this PRINTOUT9.
3. Create a query to show all the fields to find all the dogs born after 01/12/98 who were treated by Adams. Sort in order of owner's name. Name the query QRYADAMSYOUNG.
4. Print a copy of the results of the query QRYADAMSYOUNG in landscape. Label this printout PRINTOUT10.
5. Someone has put an envelope through the letterbox. It contains some money and a note, 'Thanks for treating the dog. Dan'. Create a query to find the dogs who have an owner with the initial D, and whose bill is not paid up. Show the fields PATIENT_ID, NAME, OWNER, LAST TREATED and PAID UP. Name the query QRYDAN.
6. Print a copy of the results of the query QRYDAN in portrait. Label this PRINTOUT11.
7. Edit the record that you find as the result of this query, to show that the bill is now paid up.
8. Create a query to show all the fields. It should find all the dogs treated by Adams or Duncan whose bills are paid up. Name the query QRYPAID.

Task E

In this task you are required to create a report based on a previously created query.

1. Create a report based on the query QRYPAID to include the fields PATIENT_ID, NAME, TYPE, OWNER and VET in that order. Sort first by Vet, then by Patient_ID. Use portrait orientation and tabular layout. Name the report RPTPAID.
2. Insert a suitable graphic image at the top of the report.
3. Make the title at the top of the report 'Adams or Duncan paid up'.
4. Change the font size for all labels to 12 point and all fields to 10 point.
5. Move the labels and fields so that they are well spread out across the width of the page.
6. Change the Patient_ID field to bold.
7. Add a footer to the report to include your name, today's date, a page number and PRINTOUT12.
8. Ensure that all data is fully displayed and print a copy of the report in portrait.
9. Close the database application.

Note
- At the conclusion of this assignment, hand all paperwork and disks to the test supervisor.
- Ensure that your name is on the disk (if using a floppy disk) and all documentation.
- If the assignment is taken over more than one period, all floppy disks and paperwork must be returned to the test supervisor at the end of each sitting.

Patient_ID	name	type	sex	owner	vet	last treated	paid up
111	Pippin	Guinea Pig	M	Gregson S	Hope	06/01/02	True
112	Patch	Dog	M	Smith B	Adams	28/02/02	True
113	Lulu	Dog	F	Wilson R	Hope	30/04/02	False
114	George	Cat	M	Hopkins M	Carew	12/03/02	True
115	Hazel	Rabbit	M	Dacres F	Adams	26/07/02	False
116	Butch	Dog	M	Watson J	Carew	30/05/02	True
117	Molly	Dog	F	March S	Adams	25/07/02	True
118	Constance	Cat	F	Hopgood N	Adams	16/09/02	True
119	Ginger	Cat	M	Askari H	Carew	06/08/02	False
120	Butch	Dog	M	Humbold J	Adams	20/07/02	True
121	Whiffler	Rabbit	M	Schneider J	Adams	04/09/02	True
122	Scrabble	Guinea Pig	M	Smith P	Hope	16/09/02	True
123	Prince	Dog	M	Morris R	Adams	05/08/02	True
124	Jennie	Dog	F	Wilson M	Carew	20/07/02	True
125	Blue	Budgerigar	M	Shah C	Hope	13/07/02	True
126	Dido	Cat	F	Dean N	Adams	05/10/02	False
127	Cleo	Cat	F	Dean N	Adams	05/10/02	False
128	Jack	Cat	M	Singh P	Hope	04/09/02	True
129	Fred	Guinea Pig	F	Owen B	Hope	05/08/02	True
130	Goldie	Dog	F	Khan F	Hope	20/07/02	True
131	Fido	Dog	M	Mott D	Adams	06/08/02	True
132	Humbug	Rabbit	F	MacDonald A	Carew	01/11/02	True
133	Nibbles	Rabbit	M	Rendell A	Carew	01/11/02	True
134	Snowy	Guinea Pig	M	Ryan P	Hope	01/11/02	True
135	Harry	Dog	M	Okumbe W	Adams	06/11/02	True
136	Ginger	Cat	M	Mahmood I	Adams	07/11/02	True
137	Charlie	Budgerigar	M	Lemaitre L	Adams	07/11/02	False
138	Joe	Guinea Pig	F	Jackson R	Carew	07/11/02	True
139	Prince	Dog	M	Hussein A	Carew	08/11/02	True
140	Buster	Dog	F	Wilson U	Hope	08/11/02	False

Figure 9.4

Patient_ID	name	date born
111	Pippin	12/11/01
112	Patch	14/07/99
113	Lulu	02/02/92
114	George	19/08/96
115	Hazel	30/05/00
116	Butch	04/08/94
117	Molly	15/06/90
118	Constance	12/05/95
119	Ginger	16/03/98
120	Butch	01/02/97
121	Whiffler	12/04/99
122	Scrabble	03/07/01
123	Prince	19/09/99
124	Jennie	04/06/99
125	Blue	12/05/00
126	Dido	04/04/02
127	Cleo	04/04/02
128	Jack	15/02/01
129	Fred	03/03/00
130	Goldie	04/08/01
131	Fido	14/01/00
132	Humbug	31/12/00
133	Nibbles	01/04/01
134	Snowy	29/09/01
135	Harry	12/12/98
136	Ginger	13/07/99
137	Charlie	31/03/01
138	Joe	27/02/02
139	Prince	24/06/95
140	Buster	30/08/93

Figure 9.5

Patient_ID	name	date born	type	owner	vet	last treated	paid up
201	Milo	04/06/99	Dog	Sanders R	Adams	12/11/02	True
202	Patch	07/06/01	Dog	Moser A	Adams	12/11/02	False
203	Spot	13/09/95	Dog	Barnet W	Carew	13/11/02	True
204	Barker	01/07/94	Dog	Cliffe D	Carew	13/11/02	False

Figure 9.6

Patient_ID	name	date born	type	owner	vet	last treated	paid up
221	Rover	19/02/97	Dog	Yeo E	Duncan	14/11/02	True

Figure 9.7

Selected solutions

Section 1 Database tables

Practise your skills 1.1: Books

A possible table design is as follows:

Field name	Data type	Field size or format
Stock No	Number	Long Integer
Author	Text	30
Title	Text	30
Price	Currency	Auto, 2 decimal places
Year Published	Number	Long Integer
Hardback	Yes/No (Logical)	Yes/No or check box

Solution Table 1.1 Design of the Books table

Practise your skills 1.2: Seeds

A possible table design is as follows:

Field name	Data type	Field size or format
CatNo	Text	20
Name	Text	30
Price	Currency	Auto, 2 decimal places
Available	Yes/No (Logical)	Yes/No or check box
Type	Text	5
Height (cm)	Number	Long Integer

Solution Table 1.2 Design of the Seeds table

Check your knowledge

1 Record
2 As column headings for the fields
3 Fields
4 Text
5 Number, Integer or Long Integer
6 Number, Single or Double
7 Currency, formatted to show 2 decimal places
8 Date/time, medium date
9 Yes/No (Logical)
10 Autonumber (a special type of Long Integer)

Section 2 Changing table structure and contents

Practise your skills 2.1: Books

The printout of the Books table should look like this:

Stock No	Author	Title	Price	In Stock	Year_Published
21	Jane Austen	Emma	£2.50	☑	1985
22	Kazuo Ishiguro	The Unconsoled	£7.99	☑	1995
23	Miss Read	Life at Thrush Green	£9.99	☐	1984
24	Louis de Bernieres	Captain Corelli's Mandolin	£6.99	☑	1998
25	Vikram Seth	A Suitable Boy	£15.99	☑	1993
26	Jane Austen	Pride and Prejudice	£2.99	☑	1988
27	C Dickens	Oliver Twist	£18.00	☐	2000
28	Daniel Defoe	Robinson Crusoe	£14.50	☐	1960
29	Jane Austen	Sense and Sensibility	£2.50	☑	1980
30	Jane Austen	Persuasion	£2.50	☐	1980
31	Kazuo Ishiguro	The Remains of the Day	£6.99	☑	1993
32	C Dickens	David Copperfield	£18.00	☑	1975
33	C Dickens	The Pickwick Papers	£17.00	☑	1982
34	Colin Dexter	Death is now my neighbour	£9.99	☑	1996

Solution Figure 2.1 The Books table

There should be a second printout with two additional records.

Practise your skills 2.2: Seeds

The printout of the Seeds table should look like this:

CatNo	Name	Price	Start Flowering	Available	Height (cm)
AX0293	Alyssum	£1.29	01/06/03	☑	8.0
AX0298	Snapdragon Delice	£2.05	01/06/03	☑	30.0
AX0299	Snapdragon Hobbit	£2.49	01/06/03	☑	20.0
AX0320	Aquilegia Winky	£2.99	01/05/03	☑	40.0
AX0321	Aquilegia Petticoats	£2.05	01/05/03	☑	90.0
AX0334	Aster Pink Fizz	£1.49	01/05/03	☐	20.0
AX0335	Aster Blue Magic	£0.99	01/07/03	☑	80.0
AX0336	Aster Pink Magic	£0.99	01/07/03	☐	60.0
AX0297	Snapdragon Kim	£2.05	01/06/03	☑	30.0

Solution Figure 2.2 The Seeds table

Check your knowledge

1 No, it is not necessary to select the field first. You can search the whole table. It is normally a good idea to select the field though, and search only the field you want.

2 Yes, it is safe to make fields larger in Access. It may not be safe in some other database applications.

3 If you make a field size smaller, you risk losing data. If the new field size is too small to hold the data, then some will be lost.

4 Yes, you can usually change from Number to Text. You will not be able to use the data to calculate when it is converted to Text, and it will sort alphabetically rather than numerically.

5 Only if the field contains data values of True, False, Yes, No, On or Off. Any other values, such as T, F, will be lost. Convert all values to True and False before making the change of data type.

6 The South Region database should be open. Select the Customers table without opening it. Give the Copy command, then the Paste command. Enter the new name in the dialogue box and check that the Structure and Data option is selected. Click OK.

7 Create a new empty database called North Region. Open the South Region database and select the Customers table but do not open it. From the File menu, select Export. Choose to export to the North Region database. Keep the name of the table as Customers, but select Definition only. Click OK.

8 Open the Customers table in the South Region database. Select the record and copy it. Close the South Region database. Open the North Region database. Open the Customers table. Select the empty row and paste in the record.

9 Changing the field size changes the number of characters that can be stored. It has no effect on the column width in datasheet view.

10 No, you should not lose any data. The original dates will be restored.

Section 3 Keys, indexes and sorting

Practise your skills 3.1: Books

Stock No	Author	Title	Price	In Stock	Year_Published
27	C Dickens	Oliver Twist	£18.00	☐	2000
32	C Dickens	David Copperfield	£18.00	☑	1975
33	C Dickens	The Pickwick Papers	£17.00	☑	1982
34	Colin Dexter	Death is now my neighbour	£9.99	☑	1996
35	Colin Dexter	The Dead of Jericho	£9.99	☐	1996
28	Daniel Defoe	Robinson Crusoe	£14.50	☐	1960
36	Daniel Defoe	Robinson Crusoe	£5.99	☑	1999
21	Jane Austen	Emma	£2.50	☑	1985
26	Jane Austen	Pride and Prejudice	£2.99	☑	1988
29	Jane Austen	Sense and Sensibility	£2.50	☑	1980
30	Jane Austen	Persuasion	£2.50	☐	1980
37	John Galsworthy	The Forsyte Saga	£9.50	☑	2002
22	Kazuo Ishiguro	The Unconsoled	£7.99	☑	1995
31	Kazuo Ishiguro	The Remains of the Day	£6.99	☑	1993
24	Louis de Bernieres	Captain Corelli's Mandolin	£6.99	☑	1998
23	Miss Read	Life at Thrush Green	£9.99	☐	1984
25	Vikram Seth	A Suitable Boy	£15.99	☑	1993

Solution Figure 3.1 Books table sorted by Author

Stock No	Author	Title	Price	In Stock	Year_Published
21	Jane Austen	Emma	£2.50	☑	1985
29	Jane Austen	Sense and Sensibility	£2.50	☑	1980
30	Jane Austen	Persuasion	£2.50	☐	1980
26	Jane Austen	Pride and Prejudice	£2.99	☑	1988
38	D H Lawrence	Sons and Lovers	£2.99	☐	1999
39	John Le Carre	Tinker Tailor Soldier Spy	£5.30	☐	1996
36	Daniel Defoe	Robinson Crusoe	£5.99	☑	1999
24	Louis de Bernieres	Captain Corelli's Mandolin	£6.99	☑	1998
31	Kazuo Ishiguro	The Remains of the Day	£6.99	☑	1993
22	Kazuo Ishiguro	The Unconsoled	£7.99	☑	1995
37	John Galsworthy	The Forsyte Saga	£9.50	☑	2002
23	Miss Read	Life at Thrush Green	£9.99	☐	1984
34	Colin Dexter	Death is now my neighbour	£9.99	☑	1996
35	Colin Dexter	The Dead of Jericho	£9.99	☐	1996
28	Daniel Defoe	Robinson Crusoe	£14.50	☐	1960
25	Vikram Seth	A Suitable Boy	£15.99	☑	1993
33	C Dickens	The Pickwick Papers	£17.00	☑	1982
27	C Dickens	Oliver Twist	£18.00	☐	2000
32	C Dickens	David Copperfield	£18.00	☑	1975

Solution Figure 3.1a Books table sorted by Price

Stock No	Author	Title	Price	In Stock	Year_Published
32	C Dickens	David Copperfield	£18.00	☑	1975
27	C Dickens	Oliver Twist	£18.00	☐	2000
33	C Dickens	The Pickwick Papers	£17.00	☑	1982
34	Colin Dexter	Death is now my neighbour	£9.99	☑	1996
35	Colin Dexter	The Dead of Jericho	£9.99	☐	1996
38	D H Lawrence	Sons and Lovers	£2.99	☐	1999
28	Daniel Defoe	Robinson Crusoe	£14.50	☐	1960
36	Daniel Defoe	Robinson Crusoe	£5.99	☑	1999
21	Jane Austen	Emma	£2.50	☑	1985
30	Jane Austen	Persuasion	£2.50	☐	1980
26	Jane Austen	Pride and Prejudice	£2.99	☑	1988
29	Jane Austen	Sense and Sensibility	£2.50	☑	1980
37	John Galsworthy	The Forsyte Saga	£9.50	☑	2002
40	John Le Carre	Call for the Dead	£5.30	☑	1996
39	John Le Carre	Tinker Tailor Soldier Spy	£5.30	☐	1996
31	Kazuo Ishiguro	The Remains of the Day	£6.99	☑	1993
22	Kazuo Ishiguro	The Unconsoled	£7.99	☑	1995
24	Louis de Bernieres	Captain Corelli's Mandolin	£6.99	☑	1998
23	Miss Read	Life at Thrush Green	£9.99	☐	1984
25	Vikram Seth	A Suitable Boy	£15.99	☑	1993

Solution Figure 3.1b Books table sorted by Author and Title

Practise your skills 3.2: Seeds

CatNo	Name	Price	Start Flowering	Available	Height (cm)
AX0293	Alyssum	£1.29	01/06/03	☑	8.0
AX0299	Snapdragon Hobbit	£2.49	01/06/03	☑	20.0
AX0334	Aster Pink Fizz	£1.49	01/05/03	☐	20.0
AX0298	Snapdragon Delice	£2.05	01/06/03	☑	30.0
AX0297	Snapdragon Kim	£2.05	01/06/03	☑	30.0
AX0342	Dahlia Minstrel Mixture	£1.65	01/07/03	☐	30.0
AX0320	Aquilegia Winky	£2.99	01/05/03	☑	40.0
AX0336	Aster Pink Magic	£0.99	01/07/03	☐	60.0
AX0335	Aster Blue Magic	£0.99	01/07/03	☑	80.0
AX0321	Aquilegia Petticoats	£2.05	01/05/03	☑	90.0

Solution Figure 3.2 Seeds table sorted by Height

CatNo	Name	Price	Start Flowering	Available	Height (cm)
AX0321	Aquilegia Petticoats	£2.05	01/05/03	☑	90.0
AX0320	Aquilegia Winky	£2.99	01/05/03	☑	40.0
AX0334	Aster Pink Fizz	£1.49	01/05/03	☐	20.0
AX0293	Alyssum	£1.29	01/06/03	☑	8.0
AX0360	Lupin Gallery Mixed	£2.25	01/06/03	☑	50.0
AX0298	Snapdragon Delice	£2.05	01/06/03	☑	30.0
AX0299	Snapdragon Hobbit	£2.49	01/06/03	☑	20.0
AX0297	Snapdragon Kim	£2.05	01/06/03	☑	30.0
AX0335	Aster Blue Magic	£0.99	01/07/03	☑	80.0
AX0336	Aster Pink Magic	£0.99	01/07/03	☐	60.0
AX0342	Dahlia Minstrel Mixture	£1.65	01/07/03	☐	30.0
AX0343	Dahlia Rigoletto	£1.99	01/07/03	☑	38.0
AX0356	Ipomoea Cardinal	£1.19	01/07/03	☑	300.0

Solution Figure 3.2a Seeds table sorted by Start Flowering then by Name

Check your knowledge

1 Payroll number. This is the only field that must contain different data in each record.

2 Indexing a field speeds up searching and sorting on that field.

3 You are likely to be creating small tables, with only a few records. Sorting and searching is very quick anyway, so that you will not notice any increase in speed caused by indexing. The speeding effect is very noticeable in large commercial databases with thousands of records.

4 Indexing a field causes some slowing in saving the data, and it makes the file a bit larger. There is no need to index all the fields. Just index the fields most likely to be used for sorting and searching.

5 The table will be sorted in order of Department. Where there are several employees in a department, those employees will be sorted in order of Surname. Another way of saying this is that you sort by Surname within Department.

6 Yes. A primary key is indexed, and no duplicates are allowed.

7 No. Any field can be indexed.

8 No. If you want the table sorted, you will probably have to sort it yourself after creating the index. If you are asked to index a table in an assignment, you should index and sort it.

9 When entering a new record, the database user must enter data into the field with the required property set to yes. Access will not let the user leave the record until there is data in the required field.

10 Each new record will have 'Accounts' already entered in the Department field. The user can change the entry if necessary.

Consolidation 1: Customers

Title	Initials	Surname	Street	Town	County	Postcode	Date	Value	Discount	AccNo
Ms	K	Adams	2 Green Road	Paignton	Devon	TQ4 6BL	19/01/02	152	Yes	104
Ms	R B	Adams	3 Kenton Road	Abingdon	Oxon	OX14 3NM	30/03/02	39	No	10
Miss	M	Golding	6 High Street	Didcot	Oxon	OX11 8DU	12/11/00	98	No	8
Ms	K G	Grant	1 Palm Drive	Torquay	Devon	TQ2 1GN	11/12/01	360	Yes	101
Mr	A	Hussein	2 Carters Close	Oxford	Oxon	OX2 2HH	19/04/02	350	Yes	13
Mr	N	Hussein	6 Conway Close	Torquay	Devon	TQ2 9DD	15/06/02	205	Yes	103
Mrs	D	Jarvis	11 Green Road	Radley Abingdon	Oxon	OX14 3SM	14/12/01	87	No	4
Mr	N	Jarvis	11 Green Road	Radley Abingdon	Berks	OX14 3SM	25/02/02	175	No	14
Mr	S H	Lacon	8 Norton Street	Oxford	Oxon	OX3 7BW	04/08/01	220	Yes	6
Ms	F	Maybee	15 Curzon Lane	Witney	Oxon	OX28 4GH	06/02/02	105	No	2
Ms	C	Perkins	52 Orly Avenue	Earley Reading	Berks	RG6 3BL	03/05/02	450	Yes	7
Ms	N	Quilling	32 Park Place	Reading	Berks	RG3 9SK	28/07/02	500	Yes	11
Mr	P	Schwartz	12 Wayne Drive	Abingdon	Oxon	OX14 1JD	13/06/02	250	Yes	1
Mr	V	Singh	6 Broom Close	Didcot	Oxon	OX11 7HW	03/07/01	32	No	5
Ms	H	Smith	43 Anstee Close	Paignton	Devon	TQ4 7DM	06/06/02	87	No	102
Dr	L	Smith	42 Acton Lane	Earley Reading	Berks	RG6 2JV	30/03/02	205	Yes	12
Mr	N	Smith	12 South Street	Torquay	Devon	TQ1 4NN	03/05/02	50	No	100
Dr	N B	Thoms	21 Neil Close	Abingdon	Oxon	OX14 2BN	15/03/02	305	Yes	3
Mr	S	Way	9 Station Road	Earley Reading	Berks	RG6 5PS	20/05/02	207	Yes	9

Solution Figure 3.3 The Customers table

Section 4 Select queries

Practise your skills 4.1: Books

QryAusten should show 4 records: Emma, Persuasion, Pride and Prejudice, Sense and Sensibility, in that order.

QryPriceBetween should show 10 records: Stock Nos 40, 39, 36, 31, 24, 22, 37, 35, 34, 23.

QryDexterLeCarre should show 4 records: Stock Nos 40, 39, 35, 34.

QryInstockLessthan10 should show 10 records: Stock Nos 34, 36, 29, 26, 21, 37, 40, 31, 22, 24.

qryOutofstockBef1990 should show 12 records: Stock Nos 32, 33, 27, 35, 38, 28, 30, 29, 21, 26, 39, 23. Records 30 and 29 may appear in reverse order.

QryMidPrice should show 7 records: Stock Nos 37, 22, 31, 24, 36, 40, 39.

QryCD should show 5 records: Stock Nos 32, 27, 33, 34, 35.

Practise your skills 4.2: Seeds

QryPrice should show 6 records: AX0321, AX0320, AX0360, AX0298, AX0299, AX0297. The criterion in the Price field is **>=2.05**.

QryHeight should show 8 records: AX0299, AX0334, AX0298, AX0297, AX0342, AX0343, AX0320, AX0360. The criterion in the Height field is **Between 20 And 50**.

QryAvailable should show 10 records: AX0321, AX0320, AX0293, AX0360, AX0298, AX0299, AX0297, AX0335, AX0343, AX0356. The criterion in the Available field is **True**.

qryJuly40 should show 3 records: AX0336, AX0335, AX0356. The criterion in the Height field is **>=40**. The criterion in the Start Flowering field is **>=#01/07/03# And <=#31/07/03#**. You could just use **01/07/03** since all flowering dates are given as the first day of the month. Both criteria must be in the same row.

QryCheapNA should show 4 records: AX0336, AX0335, AX0334, AX0342. The criterion in the Price field is **<1**. The criterion in the Available field is **False**. The criteria must be in different rows.

qryHeightGt20Lt50 should show 5 records: AX0320, AX0342, AX0343, AX0298, AX0297. The criterion in the Height field is **>20 And <50**.

QryAsterSnapdragon should show 6 records: AX0297, AX0298, AX0299, AX0334, AX0335, AX0336. The criterion in the Name field is **Aster* Or Snapdragon***. You could put **Aster*** in one row and **Snapdragon*** in the next row. Access will convert the criterion to **Like "Aster*" Or Like "Snapdragon*"**.

Check your knowledge

1 >=

2 <=

3 Remove the tick from the Show box belonging to the field in the query design grid.

4 Use the criterion Between 01/01/98 And 01/06/99. Alternatively you could use >= 01/01/98 And <=01/06/99.

5 Use the criterion > 01/01/98 And <01/06/99.

6 15 Or 20

7 AND

8 Word for Beginners, Wordsworth and his Poetry

9 All of them

10 qry

Section 5 Action queries

Practise your skills 5.1: Books

Stock No	Author	Title	Price	In Stock	Year_Published
21	Jane Austen	Emma	£2.50	Yes	1985
23	Miss Read	Life at Thrush Green	£9.99	No	1984
26	Jane Austen	Pride and Prejudice	£2.99	Yes	1988
28	Daniel Defoe	Robinson Crusoe	£14.50	No	1960
29	Jane Austen	Sense and Sensibility	£2.50	Yes	1980
30	Jane Austen	Persuasion	£2.50	No	1980
32	C Dickens	David Copperfield	£18.00	Yes	1975
33	C Dickens	The Pickwick Papers	£17.00	Yes	1982
87nf	Harold Leighton	Haircutting for Everyone	£15.00	No	1983

Solution Figure 5.1 The OldEditions table Printout 1

Printout 2 should show the records that have Yes in the In Stock field of Printout 1.

Stock No	Author	Title	Price	In Stock	Year_Published
30	Jane Austen	Persuasion	£2.50	☐	1980
21	Jane Austen	Emma	£2.50	☑	1985
29	Jane Austen	Sense and Sensibility	£2.50	☑	1980
38	D H Lawrence	Sons and Lovers	£2.99	☐	1999
26	Jane Austen	Pride and Prejudice	£2.99	☑	1988
39	John Le Carre	Tinker Tailor Soldier Spy	£5.30	☐	1996
40	John Le Carre	Call for the Dead	£5.30	☑	1996
36	Daniel Defoe	Robinson Crusoe	£5.99	☑	1999
31	Kazuo Ishiguro	The Remains of the Day	£6.99	☑	1993
24	Louis de Bernieres	Captain Corelli's Mandolin	£6.99	☑	1998
22	Kazuo Ishiguro	The Unconsoled	£7.99	☑	1995
37	John Galsworthy	The Forsyte Saga	£9.50	☑	2002
34	Colin Dexter	Death is now my neighbour	£9.99	☑	1996
35	Colin Dexter	The Dead of Jericho	£9.99	☐	1996
23	Miss Read	Life at Thrush Green	£9.99	☐	1984
28	Daniel Defoe	Robinson Crusoe	£14.00	☐	1960
25	Vikram Seth	A Suitable Boy	£15.49	☑	1993
33	Charles Dickens	The Pickwick Papers	£16.50	☑	1982
32	Charles Dickens	David Copperfield	£17.50	☑	1975
27	Charles Dickens	Oliver Twist	£17.50	☐	2000

Solution Figure 5.1a The Books table Printout 3

Practise your skills 5.2: Seeds

CatNo	Name	Price	Start Flowering	Available	Height (cm)
AX0334	Aster Pink Fizz	£1.49	01/05/03	No	20
AX0342	Dahlia Minstrel Mixture	£1.65	01/07/03	No	30
AX0343	Dahlia Rigoletto	£1.99	01/07/03	Yes	38
AX0336	Aster Pink Magic	£0.99	01/07/03	No	60
AX0335	Aster Blue Magic	£0.99	01/07/03	Yes	80

Solution Figure 5.2 The SelectedFlowers table Printout 1

Printout 2 should show the two records with Yes in the Available field.

CatNo	Name	Price	Start Flowering	Available	Height (cm)
AX0293	Alyssum	£1.39	01/06/03	☑	8.0
AX0297	Snapdragon Kim	£2.15	01/06/03	☑	30.0
AX0298	Snapdragon Delice	£2.15	01/06/03	☑	30.0
AX0299	Snapdragon Hobbit	£2.59	01/06/03	☑	20.0
AX0320	Aquilegia Winky	£3.09	01/05/03	☑	40.0
AX0321	Aquilegia Petticoats	£2.15	01/05/03	☑	90.0
AX0334	Aster Pink Fizz	£1.49	01/05/03	☐	20.0
AX0335	Aster Blue Magic	£1.09	01/07/03	☑	80.0
AX0336	Aster Pink Magic	£0.99	01/07/03	☐	60.0
AX0342	Dahlia Minstrel Mixture	£1.65	01/07/03	☐	30.0
AX0343	Dahlia Rigoletto	£2.09	01/07/03	☑	38.0
AX0356	Ipomoea Cardinal	£1.29	01/07/03	☑	300.0
AX0360	Lupin Gallery Mixed	£2.35	01/06/03	☑	50.0

Solution Figure 5.2a The Seeds table Printout 3

The printout of the CurrentYearSeeds table should have 9 records. There should be 3 poppies, 3 snapdragons and 3 asters.

Check your knowledge

1 Make-table, append, update and delete.

2 No. You cannot Undo the effects of an action query.

3 You can carry out calculations, for example adding 10 pence to each price.

4 If you open an action query it will run. You might not intend to do this.

5 Open it in design view by clicking the button labelled Design. Take care not to double click or click the Open button. If you do, the query will run.

6 You can append selected records using the append query. Using Copy and Paste you have to append all the records. Also, an append query will let you append records to a table in a different database.

7 A 'real' database may contain thousands of records. It would take too long to go through the records individually. There is also more chance of making a mistake.

8 When you use a make-table query you can select the records to go into the new table. When you copy and paste, all the records must go into the new table.

9 [salary]+500

10 Access has to find the other database file. You may need to key in the full file name and path, and this must be done with complete accuracy.

Consolidation 2: Villas

Field Name	Data Type	Field Size/Format
VillaID	Text	5
Villa Name	Text	20
Country	Text	20
Area	Text	20
Sleeps	Number	Long Integer
Renovated	Date/Time	Short date
Weekly Rental High	Currency	2 decimal places
Weekly Rental Low	Currency	2 decimal places
Renting this year	Logical (Yes/No)	

Solution Table 5.1 Suggested design for Villas table

VillaID	Villa Name	Country	Area	Sleeps	Renovated	Weekly Rental High	Weekly Rental Low	Renting this year
UK48	Sea View	England	Cornwall	4	05/02/01	£500.00	£480.00	Yes
UK49	Redruth	England	Cornwall	6	07/03/00	£580.00	£500.00	Yes
UK50	The Bluebells	England	Cornwall	6	06/01/03	£600.00	£560.00	Yes
UK44	Cosy Nook	England	Lake District	2	28/01/02	£380.00	£350.00	Yes
UK45	Rose Cottage	England	Lake District	6	12/12/00	£600.00	£560.00	Yes
UK46	Heron's View	England	Lake District	8	06/02/02	£640.00	£600.00	Yes
UK47	Lakeside	England	Lake District	4	04/01/00	£510.00	£480.00	Yes
UK51	Two Bridges	England	Lake District	4	12/02/03	£500.00	£470.00	Yes
E20	Mon Repos	France	Normandy	6	12/11/01	£521.00	£411.00	Yes
E21	Bellevue	France	Normandy	4	12/11/01	£402.00	£356.00	Yes
E22	Saint Michel	France	Normandy	8	18/02/03	£650.00	£600.00	Yes
E37	Villa Rosita	Spain	Costa Brava	4	03/01/03	£420.00	£400.00	Yes
E38	Villa Bianca	Spain	Costa Brava	6	10/03/00	£560.00	£500.00	Yes
E35	Villa Garcia	Spain	Costa del Sol	8	06/02/02	£600.00	£520.00	Yes
E36	Villa Juan	Spain	Costa del Sol	6	10/02/00	£550.00	£500.00	Yes

Solution Table 5.2 Villas table sorted by Country and Area (Printout 4)

CottageID	Cottage Name	Country	Area	Sleeps	Weekly Rental High	Weekly Rental Low	Renting this year	Start Rentals
UK44	Cosy Nook	England	Lake District	2	£380.00	£350.00	Yes	23/03/03
UK45	Rose Cottage	England	Lake District	6	£600.00	£560.00	Yes	23/03/03
UK46	Heron's View	England	Lake District	8	£640.00	£600.00	Yes	30/03/03
UK47	Lakeside	England	Lake District	4	£510.00	£480.00	Yes	23/03/03
UK48	Sea View	England	Cornwall	4	£500.00	£480.00	Yes	30/03/03
UK49	Redruth	England	Cornwall	6	£580.00	£500.00	Yes	30/03/03
UK50	The Bluebells	England	Cornwall	6	£600.00	£560.00	Yes	23/03/03
UK51	Two Bridges	England	Lake District	4	£500.00	£470.00	Yes	23/03/03
UK701	Bwthyn Bach	Wales	Pembs	4	£500.00	£450.00	Yes	23/03/03
UK702	Henllan House	Wales	Pembs	8	£680.00	£600.00	Yes	30/03/03
UK703	Afal Mawr	Wales	Pembs	4	£500.00	£450.00	Yes	30/03/03
UK704	Cwm Tydu	Wales	Pembs	4	£500.00	£450.00	Yes	23/03/03

Solution Table 5.3 UKCottages table sorted by CottageID (Printout 6)

CottageID	Cottage Name	Country	Area	Sleeps	Weekly Rental High	Weekly Rental Low	Renting this year	Start Rentals
UK44	Cosy Nook	England	Lake District	2	£380.00	£350.00	Yes	23/03/03
UK45	Rose Cottage	England	Lake District	6	£600.00	£560.00	Yes	23/03/03
UK46	Heron's View	England	Lake District	8	£650.00	£600.00	Yes	30/03/03
UK47	Lakeside	England	Lake District	4	£510.00	£480.00	Yes	23/03/03
UK48	Sea View	England	Cornwall	4	£510.00	£480.00	Yes	30/03/03
UK49	Redruth	England	Cornwall	6	£590.00	£500.00	Yes	30/03/03
UK50	The Bluebells	England	Cornwall	6	£600.00	£560.00	Yes	23/03/03
UK51	Two Bridges	England	Lake District	4	£500.00	£470.00	Yes	23/03/03
UK701	Bwthyn Bach	Wales	Pembs	4	£500.00	£450.00	Yes	23/03/03
UK702	Henllan House	Wales	Pembs	8	£690.00	£600.00	Yes	30/03/03
UK703	Afal Mawr	Wales	Pembs	4	£510.00	£450.00	Yes	30/03/03
UK704	Cwm Tydu	Wales	Pembs	4	£500.00	£450.00	Yes	23/03/03

Solution Table 5.4 UKCottages table sorted by CottageID after update (Printout 8)

Section 6 Forms

Practise your skills 6.1: Books

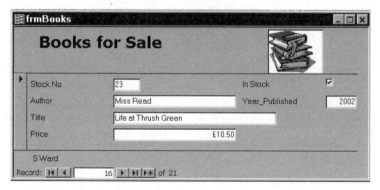

Solution Figure 6.1 Final version of the Books form

Practise your skills 6.2: Seeds

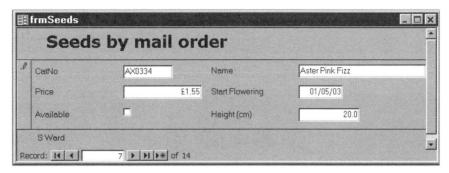

Solution Figure 6.2 Final version of the Seeds form

Check your knowledge

1 Entering data, viewing data and editing data. (There are other uses of forms too.)

2 The data is stored in the table on which the form is based.

3 Yes, you can base a form on a query. The query itself will ultimately be based on a table.

4 frm

5 Database users normally work with forms most of the time. A well designed form can help to make their work easier and more efficient.

Section 7 Reports

Practise your skills 7.1 Books

Books

Author	Title	In Stock	Price
Jane Austen	Persuasion	☑	£2.50
Jane Austen	Sense and Sensibility	☑	£2.50
Jane Austen	Emma	☑	£2.50
D H Lawrence	Sons and Lovers	☐	£2.99
Jane Austen	Pride and Prejudice	☑	£2.99
John Le Carre	Call for the Dead	☑	£5.30
John Le Carre	Tinker Tailor Soldier Spy	☐	£5.30
Terry Pratchett	The Colour of Magic	☐	£5.99
Daniel Defoe	Robinson Crusoe	☑	£5.99
Kazuo Ishiguro	The Remains of the Day	☑	£6.99
Louis de Bernieres	Captain Corelli's Mandolin	☑	£6.99

Solution Figure 7.1 Part of the final version of the rptBooks report

Available seeds, flowering July

Name	CatNo	Price	Start Flowering	Height (cm)
Aster Blue Magic	AX0335	£1.09	01/07/03	80.0
Dahlia Rigoletto	AX0343	£2.09	01/07/03	38.0
Ipomoea Cardinal	AX0356	£1.29	01/07/03	300.0
Total		**£4.47**		

Solution Figure 7.2 The altered version of the tabular report (Printout 4)

Check your knowledge

1 Presenting data for printing.

2 The query can be used to select records to be included in the report. If you base a report on a table, you print all the records.

3 The wizard lets you make choices about the content and layout of the report.

4 A label. It will display whatever you key into it.

5 A text box. You can enter a formula into a text box and display the result.

6 =SUM([Cost])

Consolidation 3: Houses

Field name	Data type	Field size/Format
House ID	Number	Long Integer (or Integer)
Owner	Text	20 (could be more or less)
Location	Text	20 (could be more or less)
Bedrooms	Number	Long Integer (or Integer)
Price	Currency	Currency 2 decimal places
Date on market	Date/Time	Short date
Description	Text	100 (could be up to 255)

Primary key: House ID

Solution Table 7.1 Suggested design for Houses table

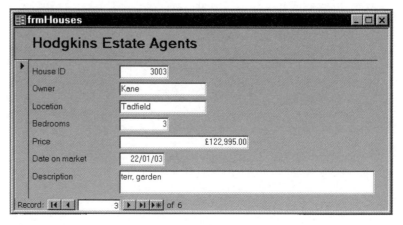

Solution Figure 7.3 Form showing record for Kane (Printout 3)

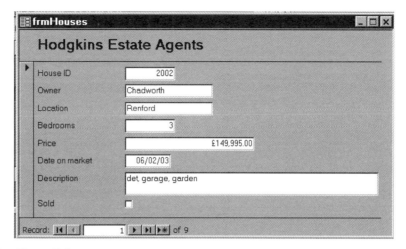

Solution Figure 7.4 Form with an extra field (Printout 6)

Hodgkins Estate Agents

3-bed houses with garage

House ID	Location	Price	Description
3006	Tadmouth	£119,995.00	semi, garage, garden
3005	Tadfield	£122,995.00	det, garden, garage
2006	Renford	£139,995.00	det, garage, garden
2002	Renford	£149,995.00	det, garage, garden

Solution Figure 7.5 Report rpt3Garage (Printout 7)

Practice assignments

Practice assignment 1: Glazing

Field name	Data type	Field size/format
Lastname	Text	20 (could be more or less)
Initials	Text	5 (could be more or less)
Address	Text	30 (could be more or less)
Town	Text	20 (could be more or less)
County	Text	20 (could be more or less)
Amount	Currency	Currency 2 decimal places
Paid	Logical (Yes/No)	
DateOrdered	Date/Time	Short date
SaleNumber	Number	Long Integer (or Integer)

Primary key: SaleNumber

Solution Table 9.1 Suggested design for Customer table

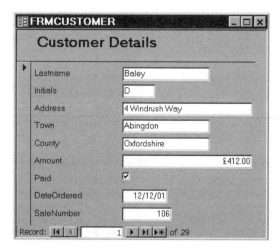

Solution Figure 9.1 frmCustomer form (Printout 1)

Lastname	Title	Initials	Address	Town	County	Amount	Paid	Date Ordered	Date Installed	Sale Number
Baley	Mr	D	4 Windrush Way	Abingdon	Oxfordshire	£412.00	Yes	12/12/01	04/01/02	106
Nelson	Mr	G	9 Akenham Close	Abingdon	Oxfordshire	£525.50	Yes	15/12/01	07/01/02	107
Goldman	Mr	S	3 Harrison Close	Didcot	Oxfordshire	£602.28	Yes	03/01/02	21/01/02	108
Patel	Mr	S	12 Sewell Close	Abingdon	Oxfordshire	£409.95	Yes	05/01/02	22/01/02	109
McPherson	Mr	M	45 Long Lane	Wantage	Oxfordshire	£220.65	Yes	08/01/02	23/01/02	110
Draycott	Mr	F	7 Hollow Way	Wantage	Oxfordshire	£378.50	Yes	16/01/02	28/01/02	111
Kimball	Ms	J	14 Frith Avenue	Didcot	Oxfordshire	£380.25	Yes	23/01/02	04/02/02	112
Cunningham	Mrs	H	63 Madison Gardens	Abingdon	Oxfordshire	£309.45	Yes	12/02/02	25/02/02	113
Sutherland	Ms	N	12 Yarrow Drive	Abingdon	Oxfordshire	£299.99	Yes	22/02/02	04/03/02	114
O'Neill	Ms	K	19 Jukes Walk	Didcot	Oxfordshire	£770.50	Yes	23/02/02	05/03/02	115
Varju	Mr	S	102 Cowley Road	Oxford	Oxfordshire	£210.50	Yes	25/02/02	06/03/02	116
Harley	Mr	D G	34 Towns Road	Oxford	Oxfordshire	£445.20	Yes	25/02/02	07/03/02	117
Greenham	Ms	K	16 Cardigan Road	Abingdon	Oxfordshire	£759.50	Yes	26/02/02	11/03/02	118
Farley	Mr	F R	15 Hookes Drive	Abingdon	Oxfordshire	£385.20	Yes	26/02/02	12/03/02	119
Murphy	Mr	S	17 Harkman Close	Didcot	Oxfordshire	£555.00	Yes	26/02/02	13/03/02	120
Perkins	Mr	P N	2 Somerset Drive	Newbury	Berkshire	£953.00	Yes	28/02/02	25/03/02	122
Cordwainer	Mr	C	22 Ratcliffe Close	Didcot	Oxfordshire	£547.30	Yes	28/02/02	26/03/02	123
Hussein	Mr	S G	20 Marlborough Street	Newbury	Berkshire	£457.60	Yes	08/03/02	27/03/02	125
Goldman	Mr	S	3 Harrison Close	Didcot	Oxfordshire	£605.90	No	09/03/02	02/04/02	127
Saunders	Ms	C	25 Cardigan Road	Abingdon	Oxfordshire	£209.70	No	10/03/02	15/04/02	128
Ali	Mr	J	29 Woodland Road	Wantage	Oxfordshire	£752.60	Yes	27/02/02	16/04/02	121
Patel	Mr	S	12 Sewell Close	Abingdon	Oxfordshire	£102.40	Yes	04/03/02	17/04/02	124
Harrison	Mr	N E	22 Marlborough Street	Newbury	Berkshire	£109.40	Yes	08/03/02	18/04/02	126
Ling	Mr	J	1 Shelley Close	Newbury	Berkshire	£886.30	No	15/03/02	22/04/02	131
Teoh	Mr	O	16 Yarrow Drive	Abingdon	Oxfordshire	£336.50	Yes	10/03/02	23/04/02	129
Brown	Mr	S	19 Yarrow Drive	Abingdon	Oxfordshire	£105.00	No	18/03/02	24/04/02	133
Anders	Mr	J	6 Green Crescent	Newbury	Berkshire	£858.10	Yes	16/03/02	29/04/02	132
Smith	Mr	F R	6 Eastern Avenue	Didcot	Oxfordshire	£709.20	No	15/03/02	30/04/02	130
Solomon	Mr	K	42 Hendred Close	Wantage	Oxfordshire	£650.00	No	18/03/02	01/05/02	134
Grey	Ms	D	24 Marlborough Street	Newbury	Berkshire	£510.50	No	22/03/02	02/05/02	135
Pauling	Mr	P	25 Sewell Close	Abingdon	Oxfordshire	£220.00	No	22/03/02	03/05/02	136

Solution Table 9.2 Modified Customer table sorted by DateInstalled (Printout 4)

Oxfordshire Sales

Lastname	Title	Initials	Address	Town	County	Amount	Paid	DateOrdered	DateInstalled	SaleNumber
Ali	Mr	J	29 Woodland Road	Wantage	Oxfordshire	£752.60	Yes	27/02/02	16/04/02	121
Bailey	Mr	D	4 Windrush Way	Abingdon	Oxfordshire	£412.00	Yes	12/12/01	04/01/02	106
Brown	Mr	S	19 Yarrow Drive	Abingdon	Oxfordshire	£105.00	No	18/03/02	24/04/02	133
Cordwainer	Mr	C	22 Ratcliffe Close	Didcot	Oxfordshire	£547.30	Yes	28/02/02	26/03/02	123
Cunningham	Mrs	H	63 Madison Gardens	Abingdon	Oxfordshire	£309.45	Yes	12/02/02	25/02/02	113
Draycott	Mr	F	7 Hollow Way	Wantage	Oxfordshire	£378.50	Yes	16/01/02	28/01/02	111
Farley	Mr	F R	15 Hookes Drive	Abingdon	Oxfordshire	£385.20	Yes	26/02/02	12/03/02	119
Goldman	Mr	S	3 Harrison Close	Didcot	Oxfordshire	£602.28	Yes	03/01/02	21/01/02	108
Goldman	Mr	S	3 Harrison Close	Didcot	Oxfordshire	£605.90	No	09/03/02	02/04/02	127
Greenham	Ms	K	16 Cardigan Road	Abingdon	Oxfordshire	£759.50	Yes	26/02/02	11/03/02	118
Harley	Mr	D G	34 Towns Road	Oxford	Oxfordshire	£445.20	Yes	25/02/02	07/03/02	117
Kimball	Ms	J	14 Frith Avenue	Didcot	Oxfordshire	£380.25	Yes	23/01/02	04/02/02	112
McPherson	Mr	M	45 Long Lane	Wantage	Oxfordshire	£220.65	Yes	08/01/02	23/01/02	110
Murphy	Mr	S	17 Harkman Close	Didcot	Oxfordshire	£555.00	Yes	26/02/02	13/03/02	120
Nelson	Mr	G	9 Akenham Close	Abingdon	Oxfordshire	£525.50	Yes	15/12/01	07/01/02	107
O'Neill	Ms	K	19 Jukes Walk	Didcot	Oxfordshire	£770.50	Yes	23/02/02	05/03/02	115
Patel	Mr	S	12 Sewell Close	Abingdon	Oxfordshire	£102.40	Yes	04/03/02	17/04/02	124
Patel	Mr	S	12 Sewell Close	Abingdon	Oxfordshire	£409.95	Yes	05/01/02	22/01/02	109
Pauling	Mr	P	25 Sewell Close	Abingdon	Oxfordshire	£220.00	No	22/03/02	03/05/02	136
Saunders	Ms	C	25 Cardigan Road	Abingdon	Oxfordshire	£209.70	No	10/03/02	15/04/02	128

Solution Table 9.3 Glazing rptSales report

Payments Due

SaleNumber	Lastname	Amount	DateInstalled
127	Goldman	£605.90	02/04/02
128	Saunders	£209.70	15/04/02
131	Ling	£886.30	22/04/02
133	Brown	£105.00	24/04/02
130	Smith	£709.20	30/04/02
134	Solomon	£650.00	01/05/02
135	Grey	£510.50	02/05/02
136	Pauling	£220.00	03/05/02

Solution Table 9.4 Glazing rptUnpaid report

Abingdon orders on or after 04/03/02   *S Ward*

Lastname	Title	Initials	DateOrdered	DateInstalled
Brown	Mr	S	18/03/02	24/04/02
Patel	Mr	S	04/03/02	17/04/02
Pauling	Mr	P	22/03/02	03/05/02
Saunders	Ms	C	10/03/02	15/04/02
Teoh	Mr	O	10/03/02	23/04/02

Solution Table 9.5 Glazing rptAbingdonRecent report

Orders over £500 or recently installed   *S Ward*

SaleNumber	Amount	Paid	DateOrdered	DateInstalled	Lastname	Title	Initials	Address	Town	County
107	£525.50	Yes	15/12/01	07/01/02	Nelson	Mr	G	9 Akenham Close	Abingdon	Oxfordshire
108	£602.28	Yes	03/01/02	21/01/02	Goldman	Mr	S	3 Harrison Close	Didcot	Oxfordshire
115	£770.50	Yes	23/02/02	05/03/02	O'Neill	Ms	K	19 Jukes Walk	Didcot	Oxfordshire
118	£759.50	Yes	26/02/02	11/03/02	Greenham	Ms	K	16 Cardigan Road	Abingdon	Oxfordshire
120	£555.00	Yes	26/02/02	13/03/02	Murphy	Mr	S	17 Harkman Close	Didcot	Oxfordshire
121	£752.60	Yes	27/02/02	16/04/02	Ali	Mr	J	29 Woodland Road	Wantage	Oxfordshire
122	£953.00	Yes	28/02/02	25/03/02	Perkins	Mr	P N	2 Somerset Drive	Newbury	West Berkshire
123	£547.30	Yes	28/02/02	26/03/02	Cordwainer	Mr	C	22 Ratcliffe Close	Didcot	Oxfordshire
124	£102.40	Yes	04/03/02	17/04/02	Patel	Mr	S	12 Sewell Close	Abingdon	Oxfordshire
126	£109.40	Yes	08/03/02	18/04/02	Harrison	Mr	N E	22 Marlborough Street	Newbury	West Berkshire
127	£605.90	No	09/03/02	02/04/02	Goldman	Mr	S	3 Harrison Close	Didcot	Oxfordshire
128	£209.70	No	10/03/02	15/04/02	Saunders	Ms	C	25 Cardigan Road	Abingdon	Oxfordshire
129	£336.50	Yes	10/03/02	23/04/02	Teoh	Mr	O	16 Yarrow Drive	Abingdon	Oxfordshire
130	£709.20	No	15/03/02	30/04/02	Smith	Mr	F R	6 Eastern Avenue	Didcot	Oxfordshire
131	£886.30	No	15/03/02	22/04/02	Ling	Mr	J	1 Shelley Close	Newbury	West Berkshire
132	£858.10	Yes	16/03/02	29/04/02	Anders	Mr	J	6 Green Crescent	Newbury	West Berkshire
133	£105.00	No	18/03/02	24/04/02	Brown	Mr	S	19 Yarrow Drive	Abingdon	Oxfordshire
134	£650.00	No	18/03/02	01/05/02	Solomon	Mr	K	42 Hendred Close	Wantage	Oxfordshire
135	£510.50	No	22/03/02	02/05/02	Grey	Ms	D	24 Marlborough Street	Newbury	West Berkshire
136	£220.00	No	22/03/02	03/05/02	Pauling	Mr	P	25 Sewell Close	Abingdon	Oxfordshire

Solution Table 9.6 Glazing rptAmountDate

Oxfordshire customers who have paid

Lastname	Title	Initials	Address	Town	Amount
Sutherland	Ms	N	12 Yarrow Drive	Abingdon	£299.99
Cunningham	Mrs	H	63 Madison Gardens	Abingdon	£309.45
Teoh	Mr	O	16 Yarrow Drive	Abingdon	£336.50
Draycott	Mr	F	7 Hollow Way	Wantage	£378.50
Kimball	Ms	J	14 Frith Avenue	Didcot	£380.25
Farley	Mr	F R	15 Hookes Drive	Abingdon	£385.20
Patel	Mr	S	12 Sewell Close	Abingdon	£409.95
Baley	Mr	D	4 Windrush Way	Abingdon	£412.00
Harley	Mr	D G	34 Towns Road	Oxford	£445.20
Nelson	Mr	G	9 Akenham Close	Abingdon	£525.50
Cordwainer	Mr	C	22 Ratcliffe Close	Didcot	£547.30
Murphy	Mr	S	17 Harkman Close	Didcot	£555.00
Goldman	Mr	S	3 Harrison Close	Didcot	£602.28
Ali	Mr	J	29 Woodland Road	Wantage	£752.60
Greenham	Ms	K	16 Cardigan Road	Abingdon	£759.50
O'Neill	Ms	K	19 Jukes Walk	Didcot	£770.50

Solution Table 9.7 Glazing rptOxfordshirePaid

Outcomes matching guide

Outcome 1: Apply database concepts
Outcome 2: Design, create and modify a database structure
Outcome 3: Design, create and use data entry forms
Outcome 4: Edit and maintain a database
Outcome 5: Sort and index databases
Outcome 6: Carry out single and multiple condition searches
Outcome 7: Create and modify a report, and produce hard copy output

Outcome 1: Apply database concepts **Practical activities**		
1 a	Identify and use: table for storing data	Section 1 Tasks 1.1, 1.3
b	query for retrieving records according to criteria	Section 4 Task 4.1
c	form for screen-based data entry	Section 6 Task 6.3
d	report for presentation of information	Section 7 Task 7.1
2 a	Use and describe data types: character or text	Section 1 Task 1.1
b	numeric	Section 1 Task 1.1
c	date/time	Section 1 Task 1.1
d	currency	Section 1 Task 1.1
e	logical	Section 1 Task 1.2
3	Make backup copies of the data files/tables using file names which identify them as backup copies, storing them in a suitably identified location	Section 1 Task 1.5
Underpinning knowledge		
1	Describe the basic concepts of databases	Section 1 Information: Databases and database software
2	Identify and justify typical applications for database software	Section 1 Information: Databases and database software
3 **a** **b** **c**	Describe the use of logical operators: AND OR NOT	Section 4 Information: Logical operators
d **e**	Yes/No True/False	Section 1 Task 1.2
4 **a** **b** **c** **d** **e** **f**	Describe and distinguish between relational operators: equals = less than < greater than > less than or equal to <= greater than or equal to >= not equal to <>	Section 4 Information: Relational operators

5	Describe the importance of file management within a database file structure	Section 1 Information: File management and back up

Outcome 2: Design, create and modify a database structure
Practical activities

1	Design and create database structures using appropriate field names, data types, specifying additional attributes or properties of the data types wherever appropriate	Section 1 Task 1.1 Section 3 Task 3.8
2 a	Modify database structures: insert new fields	Section 2 Task 2.3
b	modify the data type of suitable existing fields	Section 2 Task 2.6
c	modify the attributes or properties of the data type of suitable existing fields	Section 2 Task 2.7
d	delete an existing field	Section 2 Task 2.4
e	define a primary key for an appropriate table/file	Section 3 Task 3.1
f	remove a primary key from an existing table/file	Section 3 Task 3.2
3	Copy and modify existing database structures for use with new data	Section 2 Task 2.9
4	Save and print database structures	Section 2 Task 2.8
5	Enter data into new database structures	Section 1 Task 1.3

Underpinning knowledge

1	Explain the term 'primary key'	Section 3 Information: Primary key
2	Describe a database structure in terms of field names and data types, including the attributes or properties of the data types where applicable, e.g. field length, date format	Section 1 Task 1.1
3	Describe the impact of design on the database function	Section 3 Information: The impact of design on the database function

Outcome 3: Design, create and use data entry forms
Practical activities

1	Design and create data entry forms for screen input	Section 6 Task 6.1
2	Modify data entry forms for screen input	Section 6 Task 6.5
3	Use data entry forms for inputting of data	Section 6 Task 6.3
4	Use data entry forms for editing of data	Section 6 Task 6.4
5	Save data entry forms using an appropriate name	Section 6 Task 6.2
6	Print data entry forms	Section 6 Task 6.11

Underpinning knowledge

1	Describe the importance of user-friendly design principles when creating a data entry form	Section 6 Information: User-friendly design

Outcome 4: Edit and maintain a database
Practical activities

1	Open existing databases and display the records and fields for editing	Section 2 Tasks 2.1, 2.2
2	Find and replace the contents of fields with new entries in one or more records	Section 2 Task 2.5
3	Select records for deletion	Section 5 Task 5.3
4	Delete selected records from a database	Section 5 Task 5.3
5	Insert records in the correct position in sorted databases	Section 3 Task 3.4
6	Enter data into new database structures	Section 2 Task 2.9
7	Extract selected records from current databases and append the extract to a new database	Section 5 Task 5.1

Underpinning knowledge

1	Describe why data may need to be extracted from one database and stored in another database	Section 5 Information: Extracting data from one table to another

Outcome 5: Sort and index databases
Practical activities

1	Apply an index criterion to primary key fields	Section 3 Task 3.1
2	Apply an index criterion to secondary key fields	Section 3 Tasks 3.5, 3.6
3	Sort the records in databases according to specified criteria	Section 3 Task 3.3
4	Insert records in an indexed database	Section 3 Task 3.4

Underpinning knowledge

1	Describe and identify primary and secondary fields in relation to sorting and multiple field indexes	Section 3 Information: Indexes
2	Identify the advantages of indexing databases	Section 3 Information: Indexes

Outcome 6: Carry out single and multiple condition searches
Practical activities

1 a b c d e f	Use relational operators: equals = less than < greater than > less than or equal to <= greater than or equal to >= not equal to <>	Section 4 Task 4.3
2	Define and execute single condition searches on boolean or logical fields	Section 4 Task 4.2
3	Define and execute multiple condition searches on date fields	Section 4 Task 4.4
4	Define and execute multiple condition searches on fields other than boolean/logical or date fields	Section 4 Tasks 4.5, 4.8
5	Define and execute multiple condition searches on two or more fields of differing data types	Section 4 Tasks 4.6, 4.7

6	Define and execute a condition to search for specified characters in character or text fields	Section 4 Task 4.10
7	Use a wildcard to search for specified data	Section 4 Task 4.10
Underpinning knowledge		
1	Describe the use of a filter	Section 4 Information: Select queries

Outcome 7: Create and modify a report, and produce hard copy output
Practical activities

1	Create a report with headings, subheadings and totals showing:	Section 7 Task 7.11
a	all records and all fields	Section 7 Task 7.1
b	selected records and all fields	Section 7 Task 7.5
c	selected records and selected fields	Section 7 Task 7.6
2	Modify a report:	
a	rearrange the order in which fields are displayed	Section 7 Task 7.8
b	format fields: field width, alignment of the data, font size and style	Section 7 Task 7.7
c	insert a graphic/image	Section 7 Task 7.12
3	Insert headers and footers	Section 7 Task 7.2
4	Use print options for report layout	Section 7 Task 7.4
5	Save a report form	Section 7 Task 7.3
6	Print a report form	Section 7 Task 7.3

Quick reference guide

Create a new database	Start Access. (Use Start button, Programs, MS Access.) Choose to create a blank Access database. OK. Enter the name, choose the folder, click Create. The database window appears.
Open an existing database **Either:**	Start Access. (Use Start button, Programs, MS Access.) Choose to open an existing database. Select More Files, OK. In the Open dialogue box, find the file you want, click Open. The database window appears.
Or:	Search in My Documents or its sub-folders for the file you want. Double click on the file to start Access and open the file. The database window appears.

Tables

Create a database table	Write down the fields, types and lengths before you start. Have the database window open, Tables tab in front. Double click Create table in design view. Enter field names and types in top of design window. For each field, enter size and any other details in lower half of window. F6 key swaps from upper to lower half and back. Save design and give table a name.
Primary key	Choose a field that will have a different entry for every record. In design view of the table, select the field and click the Primary Key button on the toolbar.
Data types	Text can hold any characters, letters, numbers or punctuation. Maximum size 255. Number. Use Long Integer or Integer for whole numbers. Use Single or Double for numbers with decimal places. Currency. Use this for money. Format to 0 or 2 decimal places. Date/time. Use for dates and times and format as required. Logical (Yes/No). Use where there are only two possible values, true and false.
Design view and datasheet view	Tables and queries have both these views. Design view is for creating or altering the structure. Datasheet view is for entering or viewing data. Swap between the views by using the leftmost toolbar button or use the View menu.
Enter and edit data in a table	Do this in datasheet view of a table. Click into the field and key in the data. A record is automatically saved when you move out of it. Widen columns if necessary to show all the data.
Delete a record	Select the row. Click Delete Record button on toolbar or use Edit menu and choose Delete Record. You will see a warning that the record will be deleted.
Add a record	Add new records at the bottom of the table.
Sort in table	(Quick and temporary – also see sorting in query.) Click in the field (column) you want to use for sorting. Click Sort Ascending or Sort Descending button on toolbar.
Find and replace data in a table	Select the field to search. Edit menu, Replace.
Index a field	In design view of the table, click Indexes button. Enter index name and choose field(s) to index.
Print a table	Open the table in datasheet view. Preview first. (File, Print Preview or use Preview button.) Then File, Print. To change to landscape, File, Page Setup, Page tab, click on Landscape, then OK. You have to do this every time – Access will not remember that you want landscape.
Print selected records	Open the table. Select the records. File, Print. Click Selected Records option button. OK.

Copy table structures	Within the same database, select the table (unopened). Copy, Paste, choose Structure Only and name table. To a different database, select the table (unopened). File menu, Export. Select the database. Choose Definition Only.
Copy a complete table with data	Similar to copying structure, but choose Structure and Data or Definition and Data.
Copy data from one table to another	Select complete rows and use Copy and Paste. Alternatively use an append query.

Queries

Queries	Queries do not save data, but use data taken from tables. Use queries to sort records and to select records and fields for display.
Create a query	With the database window open, click the Queries tab. Double click 'Create query in design view'. Add the table you need. Close the Show Table window. The lower part of the design window is the design grid where you set up the query. Put in the fields you want by dragging down from the table or double clicking.
Sorting	In the sort row of the design grid, click in the field (column) you want to sort by. Choose ascending or descending from the drop down box.
Displaying or hiding fields	In each column of the design grid is a tick box. Tick to show the field, no tick to hide the field.
Selecting by one criterion	In the Criteria row of the design grid, click in the field you want to use. Type in your search criterion. This can be: The exact data entry you are looking for, e.g. Oxford A criterion using relational operators, e.g. >10 Relational operators are: > greater than, < less than, >= greater than or equal to, <= less than or equal to, = equal to, <> not equal to.
Selecting by multiple criteria using logical operators	Put criteria in the same row to link them using AND. All criteria must be true for the record to show. Put criteria in different rows to link them using OR. Only one of the criteria need be true for the record to show.
Use wildcards in query criteria	? stands for any single character. * stands for any number of characters.
To see the query results	Change to datasheet view by clicking the leftmost toolbar button.
Save a query	Click the save button and give the query an informative name starting qry...
Use an existing query	In the database window, with the Queries tab in front, select the query. Either click Design to see design view or click Open to see datasheet view.
Action queries	There are four types: update, append, make-table and delete. Create a select query first then change it to the action query you want, using the Query menu. You have to run an action query using the ! button. Update and delete queries act on the table on which they are based. Make-table and append queries copy data to another table in the same or a different database.

Forms

Forms	A form is for display on a screen. Forms can be used for data entry.
Create a form	Start in the Forms section of the database window. Choose to create a form using the wizard, or click the New button and choose an autoform. Select a table or query on which to base the form. Work through the wizard or let the Autoform run.
Move/resize/format labels and text boxes on a form	Work in design view. Select the control so that the handles show. Drag the handles to resize. Point to the control edge (grasping hand) to move linked controls together. Point to top left handle (pointing finger) to move a control by itself. When a control is selected the formatting toolbar is active, allowing you to change font, size, colour, etc.

Properties of controls	Select the object you want to alter, the form, an area of the form or a control. Right click and choose Properties. Find and edit the property.
Add/delete a field on a form	To add a field, show the field list (View, Field list) and drag the field on to the form. A text box and label will appear. To delete a field, select and delete its text box and label.
Header and footer	Drag the header or footer area to the required size. Use the toolbox to select a control and place it on the form. Use a label for normal text such as headings.
Image on a form	To put in an image from a file, place an image box on the form, then locate the file. Use the image box property to select Zoom instead of Clip. To use clipart, place an Unbound OLE object box, and choose Microsoft Clip Gallery. Alternatively use the Insert menu and choose Object.
Print a form	Print button to print all records one after another. File menu, Print, Selected Records to print just the current record.

Reports

Reports	Reports are for printing out selected data. They allow a choice of layout and formatting.
Create a report	Start in the Reports section of the database window. Use the wizard, or click the New button and choose an Autoreport. Base a report on a query so that you can select records for printing. The wizard lets you select fields. It also lets you set up grouping, sorting and totals.
Move/resize/format labels and text boxes on a report	Work in design view. Select the control so that the handles show. Move, resize or format as for a form.
Sort a report	Click the sorting and grouping button on the toolbar. Use the dialogue box to select the field(s) you want to use for sorting.
Add/delete fields	Show the field list as you do for a form, and drag a field on to the report. To delete a field, select and delete its label and text box.
Headers/footers	The report header appears once, at the top of the first page. The report footer appears once below the last record on the last page. The page header and footer appear on every page. A grouped report also has group headers and footers that appear at the beginning and end of each group of records.
Totals	You can set up totals in a grouped report using the wizard. To set your own total, place a text box in the report footer and enter the formula =SUM([field name]). You can also put subtotals in group footers in the same way. You cannot put a total in the page footer.
Add an image to a report	The method is the same as adding an image to a form.
View menu	If the toolbox, field list, headers or property window are needed but are not visible, use the View menu in design view and select them.
Close a database, table, form, report or query	File menu, choose Close. Alternatively click the X in the top right of the relevant window.
Close Access	File menu, choose Exit.